Eternity Revisited

Eternity Revisited

Messages on Life from
my Near-Death Experience

JOSEPH B. GERACI, Ph.D.

www.whitecrowbooks.com

Eternity Revisited

Copyright © 2021 by Joseph B. Geraci. All rights reserved.

Published in the United States of America and the United Kingdom by White Crow Books, an imprint of White Crow Productions Ltd.

The right of Joseph B. Geraci to be identified as the author of this work has been asserted by him in accordance with the Copyright, Design and Patents act 1988.

No part of this book may be reproduced, copied, or used in any form or manner whatsoever without written permission, except in the case of brief quotations in reviews and critical articles.

A CIP catalogue record for this book is available from the British Library.

For information, contact White Crow Productions Ltd. by e-mail: info@whitecrowbooks.com

Cover Design by Astrid@Astridpaints.com
Interior illustrations by Gerald Geraci
Cover illustration by Gerald Geraci
Interior design by Velin@Perseus-Design.com

ISBN: Paperback: 978-1-78677-171-1
ISBN: eBook: 978-1-78677-172-8

Non-Fiction / Memoir / Body, Mind & Spirit / Near-death experience

www.whitecrowbooks.com

For all the young children who have allowed me to revisit my eternity through their peace and love.

To the memory of my late brother Gerald whose artwork lives on in *Eternity Revisited.*

Praise for *Eternity Revisited*

"*Eternity Revisited* is a riveting personal account of Joe Geraci's encounter with eternity when he died, and how it transformed his life. This insightful look at what happens at death is filled with wisdom and humor; but it is less about death than about love, which transcends both life and death. This book will provide comfort to those seeking the meaning of life, and guidance as to living a life of love even in the face of hardships."

~ **Bruce Greyson, M.D.,**
Professor Emeritus of Psychiatry &
Neurobehavioral Sciences, University of Virginia;
author of *After: A Doctor Explores What Near-Death Experiences Reveal about Life and Beyond.*

"Dr. Geraci's book is a candid, caring, insightful, and vivid look at the subject which, sooner or later, fascinates and/or frightens everyone: death. His observations, descriptions and conclusions linger in your mind, percolating provokingly long after you read the words on the page. And that my friends, is the sign of a great book."

~ **Robert N. Macomber,**
award winning author, The Honor Series

"Dr. Geraci has written an amazing book, Eternity Revisited: Messages from my Near-Death Experience. Eventually we are all going to die. How great it is to be able to read one man's beautifully written reflections on his journey at death. And how great it is that he returned and chose to share that journey with us."

~ **Patricia S. Weibust, PhD,**
Professor Emeritus of Educational Studies and Ethnography University of Connecticut

Contents

Praise for *Eternity Revisited*	vii
Foreword	xi
Introduction	1
Life before the NDE	9
The Near-Death Experience	21
Thoughts about the Experience	35
Post-NDE	45
NDEs in Children	63
Joan	71
Doubt	83
Post-NDE Views of Life	109
Philosophy, Pseudoscience and Science	119
Acknowledgments	135
Epilogue	139
References	141
About the Author	143

Foreword

In the spring of 1977, Joe underwent what is now called a clinical (or near-) death experience. For a moment outside of time he entered a world of indescribable and unforgettable beauty, harmony, peace and love. In a phrase, Joe experienced the perfection of eternity.

And then he came back—back into time, place, and the imperfections of the world in which we are all sojourners.

For a long time, Joe struggled with the tremendous discrepancy between these worlds and experienced the special ache of longing and loneliness that is common to many who have entered reality, only to be quickly exiled from it again.

Several years after this event took place, I met Joe who had finally come to share his experience with me (as part of my research on this topic.) As we talked, it was clear to me that it was not his words that communicated his experience so much as it was his "being" that expressed it. I could look at Joe and find all my questions answered by his luminous eyes and the gentle intonation of his voice. In time, we came to talk about how he personally coped with the burden and gift of his near-death experience. He made an off-hand comment about his poetry—a way, he said, of expressing what otherwise would stay locked up inside of him.

Since that initial meeting, I have had the joy of being with Joe many times, especially in conjunction with programs of various kinds that we have had occasion to do on near-death experiences. He is always the same as he was at that first meeting—filled with love so tender and comforting that audiences intuitively sense that here is a man whom, when he was dying, God blessed with an infusion of his own love. And yet, at the same time, Joe gives the impression that although he can tell his secret, he can never fully share it. He can only wish that everyone could experience what he did "before" they die.

The contemplative poetry of Joseph Geraci that you will encounter in this memoir has a peculiar origin, which the poet himself never discloses. These poems were born when Joe died. In these poems of exile—which deal chiefly with his love of the sea, his solitude and isolation, and his anguish at human ignorance—you come to appreciate that Joe "is" trying to share as deeply as he can his secret: the transformed sensibility of a man who has experienced the untellable perfection of the Divine Order and for whom poetic allusion to the unity must be made to suffice.

Eternity Revisited is a wonderful distillation of a remarkable man's story of his transformation following a near-death experience in his thirties. It is full of his wisdom, his humor, and his poetry and, most of all, of the love that radiates from everything he writes.

> ~ Kenneth Ring, Professor Emeritus
> Department of psychology
> University of Connecticut.

Introduction

Goodbye, Joan, I'm going to die. That quote could have been the end of this book before it began. Actually, my death was just the beginning. This account is a sharing of my death experience, my life prior to it, the experience, my life after and worldly perceptions as a result of the experience. It is shared in the hope that it will provide comfort to those in search of the meaning of life in relation to death and beyond. It is also especially hoped that this sharing will provide comfort to those dealing with a crisis such as one of the worst pandemics in modern history. Having a healthy attitude about living and dying can help one to put both in perspective and help to manage a crisis. This sharing is not an attempt to convince anyone of the phenomenon. It is simply a sharing of one person's experience with death in his thirties and its effect on his perspective of life, behavior and attitude having reached 80 years of age.

Many of the aftereffects of the experience are not much different from anyone experiencing normal growth and age. There isn't very much I can say about the experience that hasn't been said already by those who have experienced a near-death experience (NDE) and those who research it. The difference being that researchers observe the NDE from the outside looking in. NDErs like me and many others view the outside world(s) from within the NDE and looking out. Volumes of research data echo each other with accounts and interpretations of the phenomenon. It should be remembered that those echoes originate from me, and people like me.

Through this book I add my own small account and interpretation to the current body of NDE knowledge. I feel a responsibility to pontificate on issues that go against the core values of my experience. It is not intended to be judgmental of the core values of anyone else. The death experience is my yardstick for measuring how I view the world against it—particularly through the influence of western culture. How others view it is up to the reader; please don't shoot the messenger.

Attention to the near-death experience phenomenon has received renewed attention in recent years from scholarly papers and books to grocery store checkout magazines. It has also gained more respect as a viable occurrence than it had in the earlier days of its research. The reason why, I'm sure, is due in part to the plethora of new research on the subject. I suspect, however, that it is also due in part to the expanding body of knowledge of physics and consciousness. Perhaps a renewed interest is also due to fear and concern of a change in Earth's climate, both physically and politically. A breakdown in civility and human rights will cause people to look for solutions and comfort beyond what man has to offer. More recently, the real possibility of encounters with extraterrestrials is in the mix. I submit my own thoughts and observations on those subjects from the perspective of one who has experience beyond death.

Death is viewed differently by different cultures and beliefs. It is celebrated by some, feared by others. What is considered normal in one culture is abhorrent in another, i.e., collecting and shrinking heads as a sign of status. Many believe in some form of an afterlife along with their own image of God; some do not. The means of worship takes on various masks of gods such as animals, stars, or a crashed plane in an Amazon jungle. One thing all agree on is that death is inevitable. We are constantly reminded of death daily, be it through the loss of friends, relatives or mayhem reported in the news.

A dear friend of mine, Lea Newsome, gifted me a book by Bill Moyers on the philosophy of Joseph Campbell, *The Power of Myth*. In it, Campbell draws attention to the various images of God:

> The images of God are many, he said, calling them "the masks of eternity" that both cover and reveal "the faces of glory." He wanted to know what it means that God assumes such masks in different cultures, yet how is it that comparable stories can be found in these divergent traditions—stories of creation, of virgin births, incarnations, death and resurrection, second comings, and judgment days. He likened the insight of the Hindu scripture: "Truth is one; the sages call it by many names. All our names and images for God are masks," he said, signifying the ultimate reality that transcends language and art. "A myth is a mask of God, too—a metaphor for what

lies behind the physical world. However, the mystic traditions differ," he said, "are in accord in calling us to a deeper awareness of the very act of living itself."

Nature has its own reminders of death, but it is not met with the same degree of concern. Take, for example, having a picnic in the woods by a stream. It's a beautiful summer day and life abounds. Birds are chirping while eating insects—insect dead. An eagle swoops down and snatches a fish out of the water—fish dead. A mosquito lands on your arm: smack—mosquito dead. Ants invade the picnic basket: squish—ants dead. Included are the insects on your windshield that met their demise on your way to the picnic. We won't even go into what's in the basket for lunch.

We are desensitized to some forms of death, be it animal or plant, yet they are all life. It is death that sustains our life; we need to eat to survive just like the animals at our picnic. We don't have a personal relationship or attachment to them. There is an appreciation for them and even a like, but do we love them? Human love is unique along with the emotions that accompany it. The NDE is all about that love: a love that transcends both life and death; the thread that binds us from now and beyond. It is a phenomenon that I take the privilege of redefining as an unexplained reality.

Throughout this text is a series of poems from my collection of verbal paintings. As with many paintings, they are for the interpretation and consideration of the observer. The colors are emotions and the perspectives are the reader's own. I invite you to visit some of the places and events as seen through my eyes and within

Introduction

my heart. Some appear obvious in thought but are purposeful in meaning. Campbell describes poetry as "letting the word be heard beyond words." They are my attempt to share my experience through a mosaic of imagery that simple verbiage fails to convey.

The poetry does not follow basic poetic format or style, only because I don't believe in structure for poetry. For me it is a free-flowing expression unique to the poet and not that of a paint by the numbers kit. In my early days of school, the master in my prep school (teachers were called masters) tried to show us the difference between good poetry and bad poetry. He cited an example of bad poetry:

> When love meets love
> breast urged to breast,
> God interposes
> an unacknowledged guest.
> ~ Author unknown

I rather liked it. I prefer to examine the content as opposed to the rules. In comparing poetry to painting what if every artist painted with the same technique? Would there be a Monet or a van Gogh? If there were basic rules for painting, Picasso was certainly not paying attention. Poetic license is a valuable permit and I take full advantage of it. I doubt if I will be named poet laureate any time soon. Join me in my struggle to revisit my eternity.

Eternity Revisited

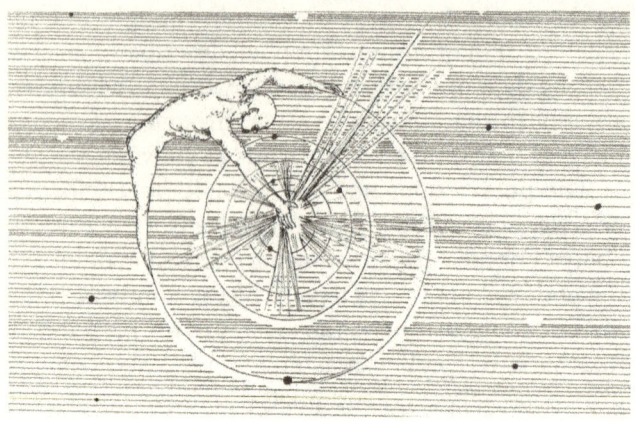

The Orbit

I find within my deepest thought
Which plummets to within,
Moments of suspension
In being without end.

I live in reverie of knowing
Of feelings to be shared,
With few who have known of love
And fewer yet who have cared.

Emotions as in music
Embrace progression for which to pass,
But love as in beauty
Needs not time in which to last.

For all there ever was
And all that ever shall be,
Is in the heart, mind, and soul
Of a child's needs laid bare to see.

Introduction

When moments pass and fade forever
How sadly we lament their loss,
As they deny us of the present
And the future is the cost.

For life is but an orbit
That doth circle about the truth,
Whose seasons in its changing phases
Seeks the light for which to soothe.

Let me love all there is to know
Let me care for all that comes to be and live,
Let me have all I wish to keep
As it's the same I wish to give.

Life before the NDE

As a child, life centered on a first- and second-generation Italian family. It was an extended family with relatives never far away. They all took part in a culture of feisty relationships between adults and tender relationships with children and grandchildren. The Roman Catholic religion played a major role in the moral fabric of the family and set the tone for discipline, with the sword of Damocles hanging over one's head. In this case the sword was the threat of going to hell, a great motivator to behave. It was also the era of the Baltimore Catechism, of which I was a victim, and had all the feelings of guilt and fear that went with it. Vestiges of that guilt lurked in the back of my mind into adulthood. The good and bad angels on my shoulders would not stop their bickering.

In junior high school we had an option on Thursday afternoons of staying in school for Manners and Morals class, which was really a study period, or attending a religious school of our respective faiths. The stereotypical Nun, with a wooden pointer that had only one purpose and it wasn't for pointing, was very real. You will pray for forgiveness or else! Forgiveness? Why, what did I do? I'm only 12 years old! I'm only beginning to like girls!

As a young man my life was full of adventure and excitement, balanced with periodic doses of pain and disappointment. One might say I was the child that didn't share and ran with scissors. The entire outdoors was my playground, beginning with scouting from Cub Scout to Eagle Scout. Scouting gave me my first lesson in spirituality as much of its emphasis was on native American culture. Everything in nature had a spiritual life and was respected as such. It was a departure from my Roman Catholic indoctrination but a spiritually pleasant one. It gave me a profound respect for the Native American culture and of nature.

Father and grandfather owned boats and had me on and in the water before I learned how to walk. My grandfather taught me how to swim: he threw me in the water! Fishing and boating became my first love and still are to this day. The desire for the outdoors overshadowed the importance of the institution of school; being confined to a desk and a room was in sharp contrast to the education received as an Eagle Scout and in the great outdoors. Most of my time in English class was spent drawing pictures of the boat I would own someday. The teacher caught me doodling more than once and probably wished I was on a boat somewhere.

I didn't do well in school, which was a source of stress for all involved. Being the first born of five boys, I was assigned a role to set an example. Neither of my parents graduated high school as they had to work to help support their families. They knew the importance of an education and encouraged it, yet they did not know how to make it happen. Sending me off to prep school away from home, football and girlfriend turned out to be their solution; if they couldn't do it someone else will. In the long run it was a good decision, in the short term, not so much.

Being away didn't keep me away from my girlfriend but it did afford me an experience with a new sport—fencing. Being a prep school, we competed against college teams as opposed to high school teams. As much as I enjoyed the sport, I was but a pin cushion for the likes of Yale, Harvard, and Columbia. That was as close as I would come to going to Yale. Our instructor was a former champion of France but was unable to put our rag tag team together. We were more interested in mimicking Zorro or Errol Flynn. I remember two of us stopping traffic in front of the gym while we dueled in the middle of the street; folks enjoyed it, except for the coach of course.

It was prep school that gave me my love for literature as that was a major emphasis of the curriculum. I spent many hours in a dark, musty library, which dated back to the mid 1700s. I can still envision the sun's dusty rays shining through louvered windows as I sat in an overly stuffed chair with my friends, Will and Geoff, aka Shakespeare and Chaucer. The classrooms were small with no more than nine students per class. We sat around a long table with the master at the end. It was impossible not to be prepared and get away with it. In my Castilian Spanish class there were only two of us and the other boy dropped out; I learned Spanish rather quickly.

Being an all-boys school, dances and social events required participation with an all-girls school. Obviously, it was met with great anticipation when buses of girls arrived. The events were of the highest social standards yet required numerous chaperons to keep everyone inside the building. They did not always succeed.

The headmaster was a kind, elderly gentleman who could be anyone's grandfather. He was liked by the students. He made it easy to like him because he never disciplined anyone. He had a disciplinarian whose sole purpose was to keep everyone in line. He was a former Yale lineman with an uncanny resemblance to the Yale mascot with a large upper frame, drooping eyes and sagging jowls. His office was one you definitely wanted to avoid.

My experiences with death came fairly early with the demise of two grandparents on my mother's side. Not very much is recalled except for a lot of people being upset and crying. I was not allowed to attend the services for either one, but I was at home for the receptions after the funerals. I think they thought that seeing a dead person was too traumatic for a young child. I was in the sixth grade when my grandmother died, however the sadness around me was overshadowed when a girl, who I had a crush on, brought over a cake from her parents. The thought that she might like me, made me oblivious to anything going on around me and it even brought a smile to my observant mother's face. My first association with death turned out to be the cute girl down the street.

High school was a turning point in my life for I fell deep into the "black hole of human development" more commonly referred to as adolescence. Life was still an adventure but it brought with it new risks and, being as invincible as any other teen, I would not be outdone. Attempting to rescue my father's boat in a storm one day resulted in my being fished out of the water by the police. I was thrown out of a rowboat by a rather large wave, which I never saw coming. The officer's stern lecture was, "Son, there's two things you don't fool with: one's fire and the other is water." That advice stuck, along with the shot of brandy for medicinal purposes.

The ocean didn't get me but a hunting trip with my grandfather almost did. While I was hunting for rabbits with him, one of his elderly hunting partners accidentally shot me with a shotgun. For some reason he thought I was a rabbit. I was short but not that short and my nose is longer than my ears. Fortunately, the shot did more damage to my clothes than to me. My leg was penetrated by one of the pellets, which I dug out with my hunting knife. When the dear gentleman came across me lying on the ground he asked me what I was doing there. Still dazed I looked up and said, "you *#+% you shot me." I never talked to my elders like that. When he realized what he'd done I thought he was going to have a heart attack. He begged me not to tell my father. I promised that I wouldn't and kept that promise for many years. Besides, if I did tell my father he probably wouldn't let me hunt with my grandfather again. Dying in either incident was not a serious concern, as that was for older people not me.

The most profound experience with potential death came years later as a policeman. I was attempting to disarm a man who had already shot someone in a crowd, then shot at me and missed. As I wrestled him to the ground he pointed the gun at my head but was unable to pull the trigger because I held his fingers back. I had to break them to get the gun away. Looking down the barrel of that gun is an image I still carry with me today. I was given a commendation for disarming him before he could shoot more people.

I performed CPR on three occasions. I was able to save two and lost one; death is an integral part of police work. There were several close calls as an officer, which I chronicle in a previous book, *Wednesday's Cop: streets of woe*. It is not for the faint of heart.

Aside from my flirting with risky adventures, girls had a high priority in my newfound hormonal imbalance. My socialization with them was limited due to my being a bit shy and socially clumsy—not to mention, acne. However, when I met the girl of my dreams in the tenth grade, there were no others, and she would later become my wife. Her name was Joan. Initially she was not accepted into the fold by parents or grandparents because she was not Italian! She was Lithuanian with blond hair and blue eyes. They considered it a mixed relationship. Once they got to know her they changed their minds, and she became the family favorite. Our lives centered on each other at an early age and provided the foundation for planning the future. Freud said it well and I paraphrase:

> Little is more exciting than one's first romance and the beginning of love in one's life. It is a unique attachment to another human being; an awakening of purpose beyond oneself. It is a baptism into the purpose of life to sustain life.

The value of education and responsibility found new meaning in my life and the immaturity of adolescence began to erode before its time. We were married at 21 and had our first child at 22.

Once adolescence passed—at least I think it did—young adulthood reared its ugly head. The early years were witness to a young couple starting out with nothing and trying to succeed. My wife, Joan, worked double shifts as a nurse and I was going to school and working part time as a police officer; all the while we were living in my parent's asthma inducing basement. As time passed I became a teacher and kept the police job to supplement our income. We seldom argued as we seldom saw each other. A second floor, cold water flat with a gas stove for heat replaced the basement; we were looking up!

The experiences as a police officer took the first major toll on my life. Witnessing the carnage and mayhem, which the human species can inflict on each other, was a sobering baptism of reality. The visual and emotional scars of rapes, murders, suicides and hate can distort one's paradigm of life and human nature. Suspicion and distrust became the norm and I seldom went anywhere without being armed. My fine Roman Catholic religious beliefs were abandoned and replaced by the ancient alien theories of Erich von Däniken and others like him. Meanwhile, I continued to go to church to appease Joan and set an example for the kids. I spent most of the time watching the clock, which was awkward because the clock was at the back of the church. The only thing I got out of mass was a stiff neck. I seriously doubted the existence of God; aliens made more sense. If there is such a good God, how can he let these things happen?

The most upsetting experiences as an officer, and most officers will tell you, involved the abuse of children. Again, how can a benevolent God allow the horrors I witnessed. I found a three-year old girl raped and bleeding; she was motionless as I cradled her while waiting for an emergency car. I caught a man raping a 12-year-old girl. One young boy had been beaten with a baseball bat by his father, who claimed that the boy had been hit by a car, all for the insurance money. Nausea and rage consumed me on a regular basis.

There were times when being a police officer and a teacher overlapped. Halfway through the school year a 12-year-old girl in my seventh-grade science class suddenly went from being an A-student to a failing one. She lost all interest and just stared out the window. I tried talking to her but she wouldn't talk and insisted everything was fine. I referred her to the school psychologist. A few days later I learned that the girl's mother was prostituting the girl. She would have men waiting for her daughter when she got home from school. The mother was arrested and the girl put in foster care. It made me feel relief for the girl in the short term but concern for her life in the long term. The clock should be in the front of the church.

There was one case of child abuse that I was not involved with, but it still affected me. His name was Andrew or AJ, and he died at the hands of his parents for lack of a better term.

Life before the NDE

Andrew

What have they done to you Andrew?
So young at five,
Your love and innocence
Torn from your future.

Your love and forgiveness tortured
Your smile and outstretched arms,
Met with anger and hate
Your tiny body beat into pain.

What parents would abuse their own?
And abuse your trust,
Assault your defenseless age
What sick mind lurks in the guise of parent?

I weep for you Andrew
I weep for all the children,
That have endured and died
In the darkness of humanity.

Despite the pain
Your last words were of forgiveness,
"Mommy didn't mean to hurt me"
Your essence to the end.

You can rest now Andrew
With all the children who went before,
You can rest now Andrew
From the pain and sorrow you long endured.

Eternity Revisited

Once I graduated college I had a choice to make, stay on the police force full time or become a teacher. I wanted to stay on the force and work in the youth bureau as a detective. I thought I would have an advantage as I held a degree in education, which was a rarity back then. The union rules at that time stated that one had to start out on the midnight shift and could only move to the second shift when someone retired; the same held true for the first shift. It was strictly seniority based. The degree meant nothing. It was possible for someone to spend most of their career without seeing the light of day, save for a sunrise. That was not the kind of life I wanted to live with a young family.

Eleven years of duty was enough; I only worked to fill in when the department was short staffed and to supplement my income. A teacher's pay was very meager back then. Earning $18 for an eight-hour shift on the force was a big help! Full time was spent on teaching, further education and advancement.

A Master's Degree in Educational Psychology and a Certificate of Advanced Graduate Study in Administration followed. My studies in psychology allowed me to put a label on much of the behavior, which I witnessed as a policeman. It also helped to put a historical and global perspective on behavior. In addition, it helped to put my life in perspective. One of the assignments in psych school, as I liked to call it, was to write an autobiographical behavioral analysis. It was an all-semester project and focused my life to that point. Much had to do with family issues while growing up—which was not very flattering—focusing on issues I had with my parents. During our weekly visit for Sunday dinner I told my mother of the assignment and she insisted on reading it. Telling her of the assignment was my first mistake; letting her read it was my second mistake. She was mortified that I would share family issues with a stranger, "But ma, I'm a psychology major!" It took her a while but she got over it. I still have that paper.

Involvement in numerous civic and social organizations assisted in my quest for the top rung on the corporate ladder. I was appointed to an administrative position and left the classroom. The goal was to be a superintendent of schools and collect as many toys as I could; a boat, camper, and small home of our own, soon became realities. Religion began to creep back into my life but there were still doubts and much of the effort was still to set a good example for the children. I was definitely still a church clock-watcher with a stiff neck.

Once I was away from the negative stimulus of police work, the focus on life became more positive and I was open to belief again. However, images still haunt me, and I doubt that they will ever go away. As I became reacquainted with non-criminal behavior, I began to look more on the positive side of human nature. My focus became more on help and prevention for young people through my curriculum responsibilities. Perhaps people's misdeeds are not the fault of God but of people themselves, very bad people. Religion, though not totally abandoned, was still not a major emphasis for me, as success and materialism were. It was all about to change abruptly.

The Near-Death Experience

In the early spring of 1977, as was the tradition, I was trout fishing with my son and friends on opening day of the season. It was a cold, damp morning and I was standing in a pair of waders in the middle of a very cold stream. In the midst of the excitement of fishing I could feel something warm run down my legs inside my waders. I thought that perhaps the cold tricked my bladder and I was having an accident. I didn't think much of it and continued fishing. It was too late to do anything about it anyway; just enjoy the warmth. It wasn't until later when I took the waders off that I found the warmth I felt earlier was blood. I had been having problems with hemorrhoids and evidently the coldness of the stream made the problem worse. After a rather uncomfortable ride home, Joan insisted that I got checked by our doctor. The diagnosis was that the hemorrhoids needed attention as they were both external and internal and, if they weren't removed soon, complications could develop; surgery was the only solution. I agreed very reluctantly because I had heard several horror stories about that operation.

Within a week I was in the hospital being prepped for the procedure; the jackknife position was the surgical position of choice. One is placed on one's stomach with one's butt high off the table with legs spread, similar to hanging over a rail. The room was ice cold and I was naked. They kept me awake long enough for me to realize the embarrassing position I was in with a room full of people. When the surgery was over I woke up in the recovery room with pain that was beyond anything I had ever experienced. The anesthesia wore off but the pain remained; pain management was obviously not part of the protocol. I recall screaming and trying to move but couldn't as I was frozen motionless in my body from the medication. I remember a nurse telling me to shut up and not to be such a baby. My responding thoughts are not printable.

It seemed like forever but I was soon put in a room for a brief stay. The length of stay would be determined by how long it took to move my bowels and pass the surgical packing: three miles of gauze. That experience would prove to be the next most painful experience. I now realize why there are rails in hospital bathrooms; they are not just for the handicapped, they are there to keep one from tearing the toilet paper holder off the wall. What was normally a rather relieving and satisfying experience was now a feared and dreaded task. I believe my fingerprints are still embedded in the metal rails. One would think that after so many years of medical research, rather practice, there would be a better way to perform that operation. My doctor referred to the operation as their bread and butter operation. Only a physician would use food as a moniker for a hemorrhoid operation.

The Trauma

Back at home, a soft diet was the rule until the wounds healed, which made for its own issues. Bodily functions don't stop because one has an operation; what goes in must come out. When Joan couldn't tend to me one of my brothers did. He was one of the best nurses I had despite my embarrassment of his having to help me to clean up after myself; I couldn't reach my butt. Having both internal and external hemorrhoids required stitches both internally and externally. They were the type of sutures designed to dissolve over a period of time, eliminating the need of having them removed. Unfortunately, the sutures dissolved before the wounds were healed. It was about ten days post-op when I began to bleed badly. A call to the doctor resulted in a telephone diagnosis calling for me to sit in a tub of cold water. Cold water is what started this whole mess in the first place! I did as I was told and succumbed to the torture but it didn't work as planned and the tub quickly turned bright red. A second call to the doctor resulted in a suggestion to get me to the emergency room asap. My wife helped me out of the tub as bloody water dripped on the floor and soaked the towels; it was reminiscent of a scene from a grotesque horror movie. Wrapped in a robe and with a bath towel between my legs, Joan drove me to the hospital.

In the emergency room she explained to the attending staff what had happened and that I needed immediate attention. They knew her as she had once worked in that emergency room as a nurse. Evidently the staff didn't believe how serious the situation was and put me on a bed pan in a side room. The nurse closed the curtain and put me on 15-minute vital signs. Within just a few minutes I managed to fill the bed pan with blood. Joan, who was now quite livid, took the pan and stuck it under the nose of the nurse. A doctor would see me shortly she was told.

When Joan returned to my room I began to feel my life leave me; the pain and fear were suddenly gone and I became very aware that I was going to die. I wasn't worried about my family; I knew they would be all right. I remember thinking that I wanted to say goodbye; it was important. With all the strength that was left I turned to her and said, "goodbye Joan I'm going to die." Joan took my vital signs and there weren't any: no respiration and no pulse. She pulled back the curtain and called for a Dr. Quick, the term used for a patient in cardiac arrest, and all medical personnel are to respond. They began external cardiac massage and injected fluids; I was revived in four to five minutes. It was during that time I experienced eternity. Allow me to revisit it with you.

The Experience

For me, life ended but not my existence; to be able to explain or describe the experience is impossible. It was not like anything I have ever experienced in my life: it was not of life; it was beyond anything earthly or biological. There are no words or emotions to adequately describe it; the parameters of dimensions did not exist, nor did time. There was no sequence; everything was at once; past present and future were one. To begin to understand the concept one must first empty one's head of anything earthly or biological and abandon all conceptions of time and dimension—an impossible task. Limited to our human means of expression, I can only describe it as a feeling of perfection, total love and total knowledge. My use of biological terms is unavoidable in an attempt to convey the emotion and essence of the experience. I was immersed in a beautiful bright light that was brighter than anything ever imagined yet soft; it was part of me and I was part of it. It was God. I cannot say it was a religious experience as it was not the stereotypical vision depicted in the arts. It was beyond that; it was profoundly spiritual. I was aware that I was always there and will always be there and that my life was but a snap of the fingers. The purpose of my life is to love; the purpose of everyone's life is to love. That may sound like something that a Miss America contestant might say: "world peace and love, Kumbaya" but it's true. The whole experience can be wrapped up in that one simple phrase: to love. Actually, you can stop reading now and try to get your money back; that's the whole experience.

Stephen Levine echoes some of what I attempt to describe in his book *A Year to Live*:

> In the Old Testament it says that we can know God but we can never be God. In my experience it is the other way around. We can experience that level of consciousness, that vastness of being, whose rapture, for lack of a better term, we might call God. But we cannot describe afterwards what the experience was. We tend to describe what it wasn't.

And it wasn't something that could be captured in thought. It was neither form nor the absence of form. It was not in time but of the timelessness from which time is extracted.

Eternity Revisited

It was like nothing I had ever experienced before but it was totally familiar.

The Near-Death Experience

Color

Color is but an earthly thing
Which serves to darken light.
Of its very nature
Lessens purity of sight.

Color in its many shades
Sets things against each other,
Yet without light they don't exist
Nor rest on one another.

A brightness in its purest form
Has no place for shade,
Nor can this spectrum ever show
From whence this brightness came.

For at its source lie peace and love
In kind we've never known,
Except but once before we came
And again when we go home.

> Color comes to those who look
> And love is yet to be,
> Brightness comes to those who love
> And do not look but see.

During that state I became aware that my life on earth was not finished: that there were things I had to do; I had to go back. With that, I felt a thud and found myself on a gurney with my feet propped up and people pounding on my chest. I became incensed that they brought me back from this place and, as I was told later, tried to punch one of the doctors. That was certainly not appreciative behavior from someone whose life they just saved.

Had Joan not stayed with me, when I was first put on vital signs, my next check by a nurse wouldn't have been for another ten minutes and I'm sure I would not have been revived. The pain and fear returned immediately; panic and confusion reigned. The only people I saw were Joan and the parish priest; this was serious! I did not have time to comprehend or reflect on what just happened to me as I was sedated and rushed to surgery to close the wounds. Later I learned that I had less than a pint of blood left in my body and close to being declared dead. I don't remember anything after entering surgery until I was in my hospital room. My family was there, obviously upset and concerned; little did they know I was seeing them for the first time. Everything was different; everything and everyone were different; they had new life in my eyes and I could feel their warmth. It was difficult to talk; their presence was what was important.

The Recovery

When everyone left, I began to reflect on what had happened to me. At that point in time I had never heard of a near-death experience. I thought that I was the only one that this happened to. For some reason, God chose me to communicate with and show himself to me. Why me? I wasn't exactly a good example of faith and belief; the church clock will attest to that. My Catholic upbringing taught that it was impossible to see God until we were dead. OK, I have no conflict with that rule; I was dead and I saw him! Perhaps experience would be a better term.

The nagging guilt I was imprinted with as a child had gone, so had the bickering of angels; Hell no longer existed. It was a tremendous feeling of freedom. The approach to life went from what not to do to what to do. However, that was, and is, met with some difficulty. Our society is filled with laws on what not to do starting with the Ten Commandments; not many on what to do, save for paying taxes.

I felt a deep personal bond to the experience; it was between God and me and no one else; it was something to be kept inside and cherished. It would be months before I would share it with Joan.

Since my experience, young children have been the personification of the love and peace I felt. The eyes and smile of an infant speak volumes on who we are and where we need to be if allowed to grow. For me, a small child and the NDE are one and the same. If you really want to feel what the essence of the NDE is, cradle an infant in your arms and gaze into the unconditional love and peace in his or her eyes. It would be so appropriate if one day the Nobel Peace Prize was awarded to an infant. I challenge anyone to show me a greater personification of peace.

I recently experienced that love and peace in the eyes of a five-year old child. It was so profound and unexpected that I can still see his face; it has been burned into my memory.

The Near-Death Experience

I Saw God Today

While shopping I passed a little boy
Three perhaps four years old,
Sitting in a shopping cart pushed by his mom
His little hands had a toy clutched tightly to his chest.

He looked at me with the biggest and brightest smile
And eyes that I have ever seen,
His pride and happiness reached into my soul
Where it will be etched forever.

His aura of love and innocence
Overwhelmed me with total love and peace,
Those brief seconds
Became part of me and everything good in my life.

By appearance of mother and child
They did not appear of affluence,
This small gift from mom
An obvious symbol of tremendous love.

I tear when I see his face
And smile in the warmth of his glow,
The personification of all that is good
And peaceful.

I saw God today
In the face of a child.

As Joan drove me home from the hospital, I felt as though I was seeing things for the very first time; everything was rich and full of life. When we pulled into our driveway there were three small pine trees that have always been there but I was seeing their beauty, again, for the first time. Once they were my nemesis whenever I backed our camper into the driveway but now they were beautiful. I asked Joan if I could just sit there for a moment to look at them. There I sat, for I don't know how long, staring at the three little trees, not missing a branch or the different hues of green. It was like coming into the world for the first time at age 36—I gained a second birthday. My behavior was Joan's first clue that something was different about me.

Recovering at home required a lot of bed rest, which allowed for time to reflect more on what happened. I had died and I was with God. He called me for a reason and he sent me back for a reason; it was personal between me and Him and no one else needed to know. In my quest to find out why I was sent back, I realized that to love is so important that if I just helped one person in my life the reason for coming back would have been fulfilled.

Although I didn't share it with anyone it was difficult to hide the emotions. Thinking about it would make me cry and, to those around me, for no apparent reason. I no longer had an interest in material things and I was not concerned with how I looked or how I was dressed when visitors came. A toga and sandals seemed appropriate. Holding onto the image of the light and basking in the euphoria of love was all that mattered. I couldn't watch television as it was so false. A simple western movie was abhorrent because of the way death was callously treated. A cosmetic commercial provided its own brand of nausea by its falseness and vanity. Fortunately, Joan had natural beauty and used little if any makeup. Turning the TV off was upsetting to the family so I soon learned simply to leave the room; my strange behavior was getting unintended attention.

Thoughts about the Experience

The experience left me with a number of thoughts that just suddenly appeared after being revived. The first thought was of total knowledge. I was aware that in that state there was total knowledge: I knew everything. Then again, my mother always knew that. She often told me I was a know it all. Total knowledge is a common characteristic of many people who have had an NDE. I was a subject in a study by researcher Charles Flynn in 1986 and had the pleasure of spending some time with him. In one of his studies he found that although an NDEr may recall the feeling of total knowledge during the experience, the aftereffect might be characterized by an increased ability to learn. He also found that the increased ability to learn is the humanistic manifestation of the feeling of total knowledge during the NDE. My new thirst for knowledge will attest to that.

In addition, Flynn found that some NDErs claim to have the answers but lack the knowledge to explain them. They claim to recall parts of their total knowledge as time goes by and they get older. One of his subjects put it very well:

> There is an innate knowledge that you come back with, but as years go by it is fed to you so you can absorb it and use it. The information comes out at particular times, in different contexts. For me, the implications of the NDE are part of the process. As time goes on, I become aware of more. Things start to synthesize in my head like I always knew it and am recalling it.

I have always had a keen interest in the theories of Einstein. I can remember waking up after surgery and thinking how little he knew. Why was my first thought of him of all people? Obviously total knowledge did not return with me but a thirst for knowledge did, in addition to some abilities. There were two instances that stand out. On my way home from the university one night, I had a vision of a small car on fire on the highway. Approximately two miles down the road there was a Volkswagen engulfed in flames on the other side of the highway. Another instance was waking up in the middle of the night with a vision of what looked like a large nuclear bomb about to explode. The next day Chernobyl was in the news. A few months later I developed an interest in quantum physics and was able to understand and already know much of what I read. I must admit it was a bit frightening. Am I smarter because of the experience? I don't know, but I like to think I am little less ignorant.

Thoughts about the Experience

Humor

A second thought was of the importance of humor. Enough can't be said of its importance in one's life. The endorphins released are a natural remedy for the many trials faced in life. It is good and healthy to laugh with others and at ourselves. Not long ago I had a young cousin who was ill with terminal cancer. He and his wife were understandably distraught. During one of my visits I suggested that they put some time aside to watch comedic programs or movies in the evening. It would be good to have a few laughs before going to bed. Whether or not that extended his days I cannot say. His wife did say it was good to hear him laugh.

I hadn't thought about it before but I realized that there are people, or groups of people, who never seem to laugh or smile. Being a *Looney Tunes* fan, I was upset when they canceled the Saturday morning cartoons because they were allegedly violent, but were replaced with sword swinging turtles and mega monsters. One has to search for the likes of Laurel and Hardy, Abbot and Lou Costello or The Three Stooges. Sorry, but they were funny; however, there is no shortage of cuss-filled standup comics.

It is acknowledged that laughter releases endorphins beneficial to the immune system. With humor being replaced with violence and anger, the role that it plays on a population in general is interesting. Could it be a factor in growing civil unrest and division? Can taking away humor from society be considered a weapon of mass destruction? I wonder if ET has a sense of humor; if not it might be evidence that they have already landed. Might be time to check some folks for bellybuttons.

One of my earliest demonstrations of humor was at a reception at my parent's house after the death of an aunt. Everyone had gathered in the back yard by the pool for food and drink. Being all-Italian, it was traditionally sorrowful and rather depressing, not to mention the abundance of basic black. After a couple of glasses of my grandfather's homemade wine, I decided that the event needed a little humor to balance things out. Without advance notice, dressed in my three-piece suit, I dove into the pool. The initial facial reactions were of shock bordering on sacrilege. All it took was one person to giggle and the hysterics caught on. Joan, however, was not laughing and questioned the number of glasses of wine I had consumed. Granted, grandpa's wine could pass for jet fuel.

The third thought, strangely enough, was that suicide was taboo: one should not take one's own life. A few years ago I gave a lecture with a young woman who attempted suicide. She had a similar death experience and never attempted suicide again.

In the late seventies, Charles Fiore and Alan Landsberg investigated the effect, which the NDE might have on suicide in light of the accounts of beauty, love and peace. Adding to the credibility of the experience was the belief in it by some medical professionals, such as Elizabeth Kubler-Ross with whom I had the honor of being part of a panel discussion. There was a fear that such positive accounts would encourage suicide from troubled lives. Clergy were quick to criticize the NDE, saying that there would be no need for religion and there would be no Easter. I suspect that there would also be a shortage of income. On the contrary, studies show that people who survive suicide return with a different message to share.

In treating terminally ill patients Ross believed that:

Thoughts about the Experience

While society has contributed to our denial of death, religion has lost many of its believers in a life after death i.e., immortality, and thus has decreased the denial of death in that respect. In terms of the patient this has been a poor exchange. While the religious denial, i.e., the belief in the meaning of suffering here on earth and reward in heaven after death, has offered hope and purpose, the denial of society has given neither hope nor purpose but has only increased our anxiety and contribution to our own destructiveness and aggression ...

In a study conducted by Bruce Greyson he found twelve reasons why a near-death experience makes one less suicidal:

1. The NDE induces a feeling of cosmic unity.
2. The NDE gives one a transpersonal perspective on one's life that helps one to deal with failures and losses.
3. The NDE makes life seem more meaningful or valuable.
4. The NDE makes one feel more alive.
5. The NDE makes one feel better about oneself.
6. The NDE makes one feel closer to other people.
7. The NDE convinces one that escape by means of suicide is not possible.
8. The NDE helps to re-evaluate one's life and place it in a different perspective.
9. The NDE leads to improvements in one's problems or makes it easier to get help for problems.

10. The NDE leads to a strong moral conviction that suicide is wrong.
11. The NDE sacrifices unwanted parts of the ego.
12. The NDE is too terrible to risk repeating.

It is apparent that there are messages from suicidal NDEs as well as from accident or trauma induced cases. These messages are not dissimilar, nor do they speak of religious practices or influence. Death emphasizes the importance and beauty of life not an escape from it.

As a police officer I had a few occasions to witness suicides and attempted suicides. The scenes are often horrific. Once a person is determined to take their own life they most likely will. One man hung himself in his jail cell with a leather strap that held his prosthetic leg. It somehow escaped the attention of the booking officer. A second man hung himself with a wire clothes hanger on his closet door. Opening the door gave me quite a jolt, I didn't expect to find a body hanging there. A third man, just 17 years old, was despondent at being alone in a strange country waiting for his parents to join him; he put a rifle in his mouth and pulled the trigger. In another incident a despondent woman drank a bottle of formaldehyde. My partner and I were overcome by fumes while carrying her down from a second-floor apartment; she survived. I was fortunate to be able to talk two people out of taking their life. In each case they needed someone both to talk to them and to listen to them, no matter how long it took. It was sad and heartbreaking to me to see someone flat line emotionally before they are dead. Life is a gift: it's rather rude to throw it away.

Thoughts about the Experience

The fourth and most important thought was that love is our purpose in life; everything else follows. There is no need to climb to the top of a mountain to seek a guru to learn the meaning of life. It is right in front of us in the form of everyone we meet, such as a little boy in the shopping cart. It is so simple; The NDE is love. Unfortunately, when something seems too simple, it becomes suspect. The usual response is that there must be something more to it, especially from some scientists.

Reflecting on these thoughts resulted in warm fuzzy feelings but they also set me up for frustration and anxiety in the days and years that followed. Since that time there have been numerous occasions where I would wake up during the night with thoughts of life, science and general knowledge. I would keep a pad and pencil by the bed, jot the thoughts down and go back to sleep. In the morning I would read them and they would make little or no sense, yet I kept them in a file, a file that now contains 32 years of random notes. These notes would not be shared until much later in life and at great risk of ridicule.

During death I had experienced perfection, timelessness and a non-human existence, only to return to a human existence with all the imperfections that go with it. It was difficult to find myself capable of hurting someone's feelings or show anger; that is not the way life is supposed to be. When those emotions did arise they were quickly noticed and apologized for. I found myself living a dichotomy that painfully pulled on my emotions from both ends. Acting human was difficult to accept. Was I at war with my DNA?

The Return

What brings me to this mode of life
Where thoughts are endless in spiraled paths,
Without symmetry and against all order
Where confusion clouds the core.

Has my constant let me go?
Have I been thrown from orbit and out of control?
Are things getting farther away?
Or are they getting closer?

Why can't I control my ship?
Don't I have the right?
Perhaps it's not my ship
And I'm only along for the ride.

Why am I the only one on-board?
It's frightening in dim red lights,
With stars as specks upon my windows
I need another with me, I'm going too far alone.

Thoughts about the Experience

It's strange how vast the universe is
Yet it feels so close,
It must be the darkness
It wraps my ship like a blanket.

There are holes in the blanket
They must be the stars,
It must be light out there
Perhaps I'm not in darkness after all.

It's my ship that's wrapped in dark
If there were only more holes that I may see.

Perhaps I'm not even moving
It must be time that tricks my mind,
Why can't I get out?
Why won't the hatch come open?

Should I sit and wait
For time to play its game?
Or should I force it open
And leap into the light?

But what is out there?
I really do not know,
I may fall and drop through time
And still be all alone.

I'm growing weary now
I think I'll take a rest,
Perhaps tomorrow my windows will look differently
And there will be more holes in my blanket.

I still chose not to share my experience with anyone. Had I shared it at that time, however, it may have explained my odd behavior to those around me. Along with wishing to keep the experience personal, there was the risk of not being believed and thought of as mentally incompetent. That was not a major concern as I was quite secure in what had happened. As the days passed, the emotions that were locked up began to well up inside me; I wasn't sure how long I would be able to keep my experience a secret. Little did I know that in the days to come, I would learn that my experience, thoughts and emotions were not unique to me.

Post-NDE

With home recovery complete and wounds healed, it was time to go back to work, which was something that I was not looking forward to. My attitude had changed; work no longer was a major force in my life; the corporate ladder seemed silly and unimportant. I no longer felt pressure to succeed: to earn a living and make enough money to take care of my family was my compromise. To my surprise, once I stopped pushing for higher positions, the offers came to me. I was promoted to two positions in one year. I did well at them and enjoyed them because I didn't really need them and was content to stay where I was at the time. I saw junior colleagues eagerly pass me on the ladder, sometimes stepping on my hands and leaving footprints on my back.

Social activities were reduced: fishing, golf and camping took priority. Although I was always close to nature, it took on a new meaning. The outdoors was my playground and I had used it rather selfishly in the past. The difference, now, was that I share it; it was no longer important how many fish I caught or how big they were as just being there was what mattered. The golf score was not important, except for missing a two-foot putt; it was just being there—the smell of fertilizer excluded.

Old places had new meaning and a beauty not noticed before. I felt a part of everything and everyone; little escaped my notice. Being and experiencing was all I needed to make me happy. It was not necessary to travel far to experience things as there was more than I could take in just around me. Joan and I were cross country skiers. Following a trail through the woods during a light snow fall was one of the most beautiful and spiritual experiences we shared. Earth is such a beautiful planet, in its prime, teeming with life from the macro images of mountains and oceans to the micro images found in a drop of pond water.

Austrian neuroscientist and Holocaust survivor, Victor Frankl, wrote in his book, *Man's Search for Meaning*, of the healing beauties of nature—a tree or a sunset—while suffering in Nazi concentration camps. He credits mere glimpses of them as one of the experiences that helped him to survive. Such a marriage of life and nature could provide healing in many of life's traumas. The Covid 19 pandemic is a timely example. Rather than looking outward in lonely woe, look inward to being one with your surroundings. It worked for me but one does not need an NDE to appreciate it. Don't miss the forest for the trees.

My contemplation of nature allowed me not only to observe the obvious but took me back in time when all came into being. I imagined the shapes of mountains being formed and thrust upward by the clashing of continents, twisted by molten flows. I drove on roadways that were cut through rock exposing eons of colored layers, which spoke volumes of geologic history. Visions of raging flood waters carving into stone cutting deep into Earth's crust filled my eyes. There is so much to experience beyond what we can see: past, present and future. I can travel without going anywhere. Joseph Campbell again:

> Anyone who has had an experience of mystery knows that there is a dimension of the universe that is not that which is available to his senses. There is a pertinent saying in one of the Upanishads: "When before the beauty of the sunset or of a mountain you pause and exclaim 'Ah,' you are participating in a divinity." Such a moment of participation involves a realization of the wonder and sheer beauty of existence. People living in the world of nature experience such moments every day. They live in the recognition of something there that is much greater than the human dimension. Man's tendency, however, is to personify such experiences, to anthropomorphic natural forces.

What tomorrow will look like depends on the extent to which man interferes with the natural order of things. My reluctance to travel far was not shared by those close to me. Yet I am:

Eternity Revisited

I am the sun's ray lost in oceans deep
The tree that to the gale bows,
The cold rain that in earth's warmth does keep
The child's tear on a mother's brow.

I am the mist resting on mountain high
The frozen earth that keeps life's seed,
The passion lost in a lover sigh
The clenching hand of a child in need.

I am fresh fallen snow on a sleeping fern
The rolling blue tides that caress the beach,
The cool zephyr neath the wing of a tern
The sad sorrow of life and the warm love of peace.

I am each grain of sand that softens earthy shores
I am joy that shines bright, I am peace that shines true,
I am everything and nothing more
I am you.

Post-NDE

Sharing the Experience

Time was running out on my ability and desire to keep my experience a secret: an eruption was imminent. One summer weekend we were camping in Vermont as a family. Joan and I put the children to bed and sat by the campfire with a glass of wine, a starlit sky and the crackling glow of a fire. This was the perfect opportunity to tell Joan what happened six months ago in the hospital. It was a risk but I had to take it. I opened my mouth and nothing came out but sobs and crying; I was an uncontrollable blob whose tears almost put the fire out. For Joan it was another puzzling behavior in what has become the norm rather than the exception. She was comforting and made no attempt to pressure me into an explanation. Determined to speak I forced it out sentence by sentence punctuated by burst of sobs and tears. "When the doctors and nurses tried to revive me in the hospital, I was dead ... I was with God, I was part of him and he was part of me ... It was total love and peace, there was no time, everything was all at once ... I felt that I was always there and always will be there, that my life was just a snap of the fingers ... I didn't want to come back but I became aware that I had to, that it wasn't my time yet. I had things to do ... I still didn't want to come back ... I knew you and the children would be ok ... The light was so bright yet so beautiful; the whole experience was unlike anything experienced in my life: it wasn't of this earth; I can't explain it or put it into words: you would have to crawl into my head to feel what it was like ... I'm trying to hold on to that perfection but it's hard ... it's hard being human again."

Joan took my hands into hers and, with tears in her own eyes, said she believed me and that she wanted to know more about it; the weight of the world had been lifted from my shoulders. We sat there for a long time with our arms around each other in silence staring at the fire. After that night we talked freely about the experience; she wanted to learn as much as she could and I needed to talk about it. Her support and understanding helped to free me from myself and readjust to my roles as husband and father. Part of this manuscript is being written at that same campground 57 years later, alone.

Freedom

It's strange how freedom comes
Alight on wings of sorrow,
Above the pall of hurt
Thrown into all that's new.

Yet that which is quickly gone
Pulls hard within the heart,
Ties that were securely bound
Stretch beyond their time.

As one by one they break
The pain recoils within,
They leave me less than what I was
Lighter I float away.

It's strange how freedom comes
As though in hopelessness it's born,
Like a sparrow lost at sea
That finds a log on which to ride.

Eternity Revisited

> Somewhere in this vastness
> Is a place where I can rest,
> Something that will take the place
> Of all I left behind.

The second person I was able to share the experience with was our parish priest who was like a father to me. He listened intently as I shared my experience. I thought for sure I was going to get kicked out of the church. Strangely enough he just smiled as though he knew what I was talking about. I told him I could no longer identify with much of the religious rote or symbolism. I did not feel a need to join in a repetitious chorus of chants. All that mattered was to live a life of love without the window dressing. The Catholic church did not have a corner on the love market.

I did admit that I found peace and love in the meaning of the mass and the church was a comforting place to connect. I did respect those who worshiped as they did, since it worked for them and I was no one to judge how they expressed their faith. I do have a bit of an issue with some religious practices that border on commercialism and entertainment. Some appear to be cult-like in nature with overly strict rules for compliance. And financial support. Again, how people choose to worship is up to them and what is in their hearts. It should not, however, be to feed someone's ego or savings account.

I could still attend church and, at the same time, be comfortable in my experience; the common essence was there. I told him I didn't feel the need to attend church regularly as I carry my church with me every day wherever I go and guilt is not my trip. I thought for sure that would do it. Instead, he made me a Eucharistic

Minister. Being a priest short in the parish, he gave me additional duties in caring for the sick and elderly. Among my responsibilities was using my lunchtime to bring communion to parishioners in convalescent homes and hospitals. It gave my love a real purpose. He knew what he was doing.

A few months after our camping trip, I felt confident enough to, once again, share the experience with two very close friends. They were both understanding and skeptical with a good dose of humor. One claimed that he was still waiting for me to return from the experience or, as he put it, the dead. One said he couldn't tell the difference in me and that I couldn't even die right. I had a reputation of being quiet and laid-back. The humor was important, welcomed and shared. One of them was a short fellow and often times when he was speaking at a table I would tell him to stand up, knowing that he was already standing up.

Another colleague informed me that he read of a researcher at the University of Connecticut who was studying experiences that people had while they were clinically dead. He referred to them as near-death experiences. There was an article in the magazine section of the Sunday paper, which he shared with me regarding his research. It was now clear that I was not the only one on earth who'd had this experience; there is a whole group of us running around! The researcher's name was Dr. Kenneth Ring. My friend and I were both taking courses at the university and he suggested that I stop in to see him and share my story with him. I was reluctant at first as I felt that there was no need to share it further.

Numerous times on campus I would walk by his building and get the urge to go in and introduce myself but always managed to resist the temptation. One day, as if drawn, I found myself knocking on his office door. He answered and I, feeling like an embarrassed child, stumbled through my introduction. Little did I know at that moment I was looking at someone who was to become one of my best friends and a mentor. His warmth and sincerity were so profound that I wondered if he also had an experience like mine as he exuded much of the feelings I had come to know.

After sharing my experience with him, we maintained contact. He asked if I would give a presentation to his class at the university; reluctantly I agreed because I wasn't sure I could control my emotions. Sharing the experience at a public forum along with the emotions was difficult but, after several lectures, I began to accept being emotional: it was part of the experience and so be it.

Through Ken I proceeded from class talks to a documentary and on to TV talk shows promoting his latest book. The documentary was the baptism of my media experiences. It was a documentary that thirty years later would come to the attention of a rock musician in England. It led to the cooperation of two albums, one with a sound bite of my experience from the documentary and the other a cooperative effort with his music and my poetry as lyrics titled *The Passage*. The latter was popular in Europe and the East but not very popular in the U.S. It didn't fit into the Western rock culture. Its meditative nature was welcomed elsewhere.

Prior to taking part in the documentary, I was quite nervous at the prospect of meeting other people who'd had a similar experience. What would we say to each other? How would we act? To my astonishment, there was no need to say anything or do anything. It was comforting to look into someone's eyes and feel complete understanding; there was no need to verbalize, we just knew: very similar to the communication during the NDE. The radiance of the NDE was there. The only conversations that took place were about families and work. The bonds made that day would last for years.

Radio and TV talk shows were mostly positive experiences; being treated like a mini-celebrity was both exciting and disappointing. It was exciting because of meeting new and famous people but it was disappointing in that there was never enough time to adequately discuss the subject. Not being able to discuss it fully would lead to more questions than answers, confusion and misinterpretation.

One of the more memorable experiences was being a panel guest on the Phil Donahue Show. During the question-and-answer period, a woman stood up in the back of the audience, waving a bible and, in an admonishing tone, spoke of hell and damnation. Evidently all this talk about love and the beauty of the experience left no room for a discourse on Hell and evil and she wanted to know what we had to say about it. Mr. Donahue turned to the panel and asked who wants to answer that one! After a brief hesitation I volunteered. I told the woman that I could not identify with the concept of Hell and that the God I have come to know is incapable of sending someone to an eternity of pain and suffering; it did not compute. I went on to explain that there is love or the absence of it: hate and evil is not acknowledged. The worst death would be to die and not experience what I did; simply to die and cease to exist. Sounds of approval came from the audience and the woman sat down. I believed in what

I said. I do not believe in hell or the devil: believing in them is what allows them to exist in one's mind and serves as an excuse for one's lack of love.

As time went on, I learned to be selective in choosing what venues to share the NDE. On one occasion some of us were duped into filming a documentary by an independent producer. Nothing seemed out of the ordinary with the interviews and the locations. When the taping was finished we were told that we would be informed when it would be aired on TV. It turned out that it was aired on Halloween night and narrated by Vincent Price. Although I am a fan of Mr. Price, it obviously did nothing to help the understanding of the NDE. Meeet Joooe Geraaaaci ...

A second questionable interview took place with a local TV station. In their attempt to sensationalize the phenomenon of a light at the end of a tunnel, they drove through an actual tunnel. The only problem was that it included the fluorescent lights on the roof of the tunnel. Actually, I thought it was quite funny.

On yet another humorous note, Ken and I were sitting on the set of the *Today Show* waiting to be interviewed by Tom Brokow. I thought I would ease the nervousness and turned to Ken and said, "let's have some fun: just when Tom introduces me as a near-death survivor I'll slump over and slide off the chair!" I almost gave Ken an NDE! Like I said, it's important to have a sense of humor but it's not always appreciated.

During one speaking engagement I noticed that the audience was quite pensive. I suspected that the subject of a near-death experience was to be a somber event. When I was introduced, I started by saying, "Hi, I'm the dead guy you came to hear." That was the end of pensiveness: laughter took care of that.

Post-NDE

In 2013 I gave a presentation on the NDE at TEDx in Wilmington, Delaware. I was honored to be asked but unusually nervous at the same time. I was given ten minutes to describe eternity with no time for questions. I am not used to structure for an unstructured topic. The reviews were many and mixed; it was not my best effort in trying to explain the phenomenon.

Lectures and talks on the phenomenon were more appropriate as they lent themselves to personal interaction and time for questions and answers. Eye contact and expressions made a big difference. One question I am often asked is if I was afraid to die. My response has always been yes, dying is a process which can be frightening and painful. If you ask if I am afraid of death, the answer is no. Joan did a study, for an advanced nursing degree, of NDErs and how their loss of the fear of death related to their wellness. She found that:

> Losing the fear of death can avoid many crisis-type situations. This is shown when the near-death survivor is admitted to the acute care hospital for a complete assessment and eventual open-heart surgery. Loss of the fear of death keeps one from developing many of the anxieties associated with surgery. It will allow for a higher level of wellness to take place in the emotional responses to the situation and the nurse will meet with less resistance and frustrations, therefore, establishing a better relationship with the nurse and other members of the health team. Attitudes will be more positive because of this loss of fear of death and will greatly increase chances of survival.

Those findings are quite appropriate today in light of the Covid 19 pandemic.

The greatest risk of all was the belief of some that you were weird or just plain crazy. One person that I gave a lecture with was abandoned by her husband and children because she embarrassed them by speaking publicly about her experience; they also thought she lost her mind. I was fortunate in that I had the support of my family and if anyone thought I was weird they didn't share it with me.

Running in parallel to the public experiences was assisting with a chapter of the International Association of Near-Death Studies (IANDS). One meeting took place in the living room of our home with Ken and my good friend Dr. Bruce Greyson head of the psychiatry department of the University of Connecticut Health Center. Bruce is as warm and empathetic as Ken. I was now involved with two of the most prominent researchers on what was now widely known as a near-death experience.

It is interesting to note that I first heard that term NDE from Ken, on a trip to Boston to appear on a TV talk show. I questioned why he called it a near-death experience because as far as I was concerned there was nothing near about it, it was death. After a brief tête-à-tête he explained that most researchers would not buy into the concept of complete death—if one were dead they wouldn't be back—it was an attempt to make the phenomenon more credible to the scientific and medical communities. We agreed to disagree and left it at that, for now.

I have since taken the privilege of re-coining the term to After Death Experience (ADE). Levine, author of *A year to live*, would disagree with me. He believes it should be called After Dying or During Death

Experiences. An After Death Experience would be a rebirth. Semantics aside I will continue to refer to the phenomenon, unexplained reality, as the NDE in a reluctant effort to continue to appease some in the scientific community. For the NDE community it will be the ADE. One day the melding of the physical and metaphysical will define and prove the ADE. In the meantime, I doubt that it will change the narrative but it is my attempt to open the door. I also doubt if IANDS is about to change their stationary any time soon.

The term death refers only to the cessation of life as we know it: it is not a termination of existence. Many NDErs say they had to return as they had more to do; return from where? There! Return to where? Here! One can't be there and here at the same time; or maybe one can.

Since the term NDE came into existence, much has evolved in science and technology. Laws of physics are being questioned, knowledge of the cosmos has expanded exponentially, and the theoretical concepts of time, space and dimensions are being challenged. Levels of consciousness are being seriously researched and redefined. It would be a disservice to the expansion of knowledge to assume that death is a finality. The theory of quantum tunneling is a good start. Despite the stubbornness in some circles I still maintain that the Earth is not flat.

Support

A support group was established by Bruce Greyson at the University of Connecticut Health Center. The group was a great success as it provided support not only for people who had a near-death experience but for their family and friends as well. Joan and I always went to the meetings together, which kept us strong and close. Her interest in the experience caused her to use the subject in her research papers as she pursued graduate degrees in nursing. Bruce guided the sessions in a manner which provided for a relaxed comfort level and it continued that way long after Bruce had left. Many participants took comfort in knowing that they were not insane and that they shared in a phenomenon that was experienced by many people around the world. It was also important for friends and relatives of NDErs to understand that they were not the same people they once were, and that their values had changed. In the case of married couples who were attracted to each other for certain traits and values, it can be traumatic when one of those people is no longer the "attracted" person. It is as if one is suddenly married to a different person and, unfortunately, not everyone survives the transition; divorce is not uncommon.

Supporting a person who has experienced an NDE sometimes requires empathy and compassion, not necessarily understanding, as it is hard to understand something that can't be explained. To treat them as being unstable is not supportive and only alienates them. There are groups that encourage the support of significant others who have experienced alcoholism, drug addiction, criminal behavior or emotional changes; why should the NDEr not be entitled to a support group? They did not experience any of the above afflictions: they experienced peace and love. If anything, they could provide support to their significant others. We could all benefit from a lesson on using peace and love in our lives. Don't shun them, learn from them. It is as much support for significant others as for the experiencer.

One of the problems with a support group is in the sharing of feelings and emotions. Friends and relatives are able to express their feelings and concerns toward their loved ones but the NDEr is often incapable of expressing something for which there are no words. Some compensate through emotions or deeds but for me my expression came in the form of poetry; not in the words but in the emotions of love, sorrow and anguish that they bring. As beautiful as the NDE is, living life afterward can be quite difficult. A fellow NDEr once said that it was actually a curse. All things being equal I cannot consider it to be a curse as the beauty of the experience far outweighs any negative side effects. Sometimes, however, all things are not equal and the pressures of life and relationships can overwhelm the purest of desires and intentions.

There are times when people who hear you talk about the experience expect a higher form of behavior from you. When that falls short, they test or question the validity of things you said and doubt that you had such an experience. On more than one occasion I have been told, "For someone with a Ph.D., you're pretty stupid" or "How can you do that when you say the opposite?" That hurts but it's part of the risk of sharing. Siblings who have known you all their lives find it difficult to see you in any other way than they knew you before the event. One may change on the inside but the outside appearance is the same. You may always be the bossy big brother or know it all. Issues between siblings don't go away because one has changed, it's because they haven't. You're not a real doctor.

Aside from the support group, my family also took part in many of my interviews with the media.

They shared their views on my experience and how it changed my attitude and behavior. In some respects my family underwent some changes themselves. It reemphasized the importance of caring in their lives with family and friends. Everyone took ownership of it, which allowed me the freedom to express myself and share what I could.

NDEs in Children

As time went on, sharing my experience became less frequent allowing me to settle back into a relatively normal life. The experience became a research project in the form of a doctoral dissertation; "Student's Post Near-Death Experience: Attitude and Behavior toward Education and Learning." It was a study that focused on adults who had an NDE when they were a child, and, looking back, how they felt it had affected them with their schooling. Many researchers have addressed the NDEs in children and found them much like those of adults. The articulation of the experience varied according to age. Some studies dealt with their experiences with teachers, school and conflicts, as a result of an uninformed educational system with respect to the NDE. There has been no specific research on how a childhood NDE changes the attitude and behavior of the experiencer with respect to schooling or problems with adjustment recalled later in life.

The subjects ranged in age from five to thirteen years old at the time of their NDE and they lived in many different states in the US. It was difficult to remain objective during the study as many of their accounts and observations reflected my own. Attention had to be maintained to a strict protocol. The trauma leading up to their NDE was varied. As an educator and an NDEr, I was curious about how the NDE affected the lives of students. I suspected that there was a very large, underserved population in our schools. I felt a strong obligation to find out and address it.

One participant was nine years old at the time of her NDE as a result of a seizure. She claimed that prior to her experience, she had very low self-esteem due to a dysfunctional family. Post NDE she felt good about herself and knew she was O.K.

A seven-year-old boy lost consciousness from a tonsillectomy in 1945. He told his father of his experience and that he saw a man walking on the moon. He also had a sudden interest and knowledge of chemistry. His father became upset and told him not to tell his mother because she is easily upset.

A six-year-old girl, also from a dysfunctional family, had her NDE while learning how to swim. Her older brother decided to show her how to swim the same way her mother learned. If it was good enough for her mother it was good enough for her. He tied a rope around her waist and towed her behind a boat. It wasn't long before the force of the water filled her lungs. She could see her body from above and was detached from it. She heard voices telling her she had to go back, that this shouldn't have happened, and she was revived. Since then, she no longer bought into the dysfunction of her family. Although she found humanity confusing, she felt overwhelming love for everyone. In her adult life she was a hospital volunteer for the terminally ill.

One account was relayed with a healthy dose of humor. A seven-year-old boy was staying on his uncle's farm during the summer. A thunderstorm was approaching and his uncle told him to cut the cow loose that was tethered to a tree in the field. Eager to save the cow he grabbed a metal tub from the porch to shield him from the rain and ran about 15 feet barefoot when he was struck by lightning. It threw him 230 feet away. He had his NDE as he lay motionless in the hospital for three days. He said the NDE was a wonderful experience and he was glad that he had it. New things about the experience unfold to him every day.

A ten-year-old boy reminded me of myself in a way. He was in a rock fight, with other boys, which was like a game I played with my brother. We would stand on opposite sides of a brook and try to splash each other by throwing rocks in the water. In this case, however, they were throwing rocks at each other when one struck him on the head. He didn't give his NDE much thought once he regained consciousness. As the years went on, knowledge from the experience began to surface. He became a policeman and produced a documentary on the NDE.

A second drowning victim was an eight-year-old boy who got caught in an undertow. He admitted having an NDE and responded to post NDE questions but did not want to discuss details of the experience; it was too personal.

A boy in kindergarten was a third drowning victim. He saw himself sink, surrounded by blackness, and saw his bubbles going toward the light. Once revived, he had no fear and things were different; but he knew something wasn't right.

Apparently, dangerous games among children are not that uncommon. One thirteen-year-old and a friend were pretending to choke each other in the school cafeteria. When the one being choked began gasping for air his friend thought he was joking and kept it up. The boy fell into a state of complete nothingness, total darkness, neither warm nor cold. He had no fear, worries or cares, just a peace that he never felt before. A bright circle of light appeared and in it was his lifeless body; he was no longer a physical being. There was no sense of time and everything was in one place. When he was revived he was told that he was unconscious for a couple of seconds. At the time of my study he was working on his third Ph.D.

I found it interesting, as other researchers have, how young children who experience an NDE can recall events in detail. One eight-year-old girl fell and hit her head on a coffee table. She was able to recall, in color, every significant event in her life up to that point.

The studied subjects were asked a series of questions on their attitude and behavior toward their education as a result of their experience. Some of the results of the study showed the following: When questioned about their attitude toward school, they had a high level of desire to help others, with compassion, listening, patience, understanding and acceptance. They wanted that from their teachers as well. As one woman said, she wanted more teachers and less educators. All respondents had a low level of interest in rewards and academic achievement. Good behavior was important but not that important.

In expressing their behavior toward their education, a majority had high levels of interest in course selection. They wanted only what they were interested in and not what a set curriculum dictated. Many believed in the importance of a long attention span. Low on their list of priorities was the importance of a daily schedule, the completion of assignments, meeting deadlines and attendance.

There was no clear preference of one class subject over another as their choices were based on individual interests. A common trait among all of them was an emphasis on humanitarian concerns. Any adjustment problems in school were attributed to adjustment problems with life in general. As a result of their experience, some felt detached or withdrawn in school as if from another world; they had a thirst for knowledge that the traditional school routine did not fulfill. Some did not see their adjustment as a problem and claimed it made them more pronounced and confident; school was not adjusting to them. Often, they were part of the silent population who sat quietly in the back of the room.

The research also showed that young NDErs wanted to expand their knowledge beyond what was required and not be judged. They were an independent lot. They also performed well on personal issues vs. conformity. Conformity was expressed with indifference, detachment and lack of interest. Like adults, me included, they do not like being told what they can't do; they would rather be told what they may do. It is interesting to note that the NDE student's inability to conform often manifests itself in behavior similar to a learning-disabled child. Some respondents claimed that they were regarded as dumb, stupid and socially retarded. If the child chooses not to share his or her NDE, it is possible for them to go through school with such a label and be placed by academic institutions into what they believe is an appropriate group: a frustrating experience at the very least. One must keep in mind the profound knowledge and insight that many people feel after the experience and imagine being labeled as learning disabled and treated as such, again from an uninformed education system.

Many subjects spoke of their expanded knowledge and interest in people; they also spoke of being more spiritual than religious and accepting of other's views and practices. It is also interesting to note that the aftereffects of their experience, even from an early age, last a lifetime and the memory is as vivid as if it happened that very day.

To date, no formal process exists to identify such students since the NDE phenomenon is not acknowledged as a cause of apparent dysfunctional educational behavior. Nor is there a process to identify these students for gifted and talented programs as well. Often, young children have difficulty in expressing their experience. They do not have the articulation or audience that an adult has. Subsequently, they are less likely to risk ridicule in trying to explain it. It is up to educators to educate themselves on the phenomenon, its characteristics and how to address it.

Educators like to advocate critical thinking, questioning and exploration yet fail to practice what they expect students to do. This author's attempt to provide an in-service, in his own school district on the subject and his research, met with almost zero interest. Out of over 500 teachers only one signed up for the workshop. Until this phenomenon is recognized as a legitimate source and reason for human behavior, these children will continue to be treated and categorized far from their potential. Whether or not one believes in the phenomenon is not the issue; it is a real and significant event in one's life with a lasting impact on behavior. To ignore it because of fear or ignorance is a disservice to the education profession and the NDE population of children they are serving.

I learned long ago that many students fall through the cracks and do not fit the norm whether it's an NDE student or not. I experienced one phenomenon with teachers when I was still on the force and working toward a bachelor's degree. One of my instructors asked if I would give a talk on juvenile delinquency to his graduate class of teachers; I agreed. I decided to back up my talk with photographs from the department's ID bureau. Some of the photographs were quite graphic, perhaps too graphic. I wanted to show them some of the things that some of their students were subjected to once they left school for the day. Many of the accounts involved drugs, fights, sexual- and physical abuse and, in some cases, suicide.

Their reaction was one of total denial. They accused me of making up stories despite the photographs. One called me a liar; a few walked out. They had obviously led very sheltered lives. What I found most disturbing was that they were obviously not the ones that a student with an issue would be going to for advice or help. That was years ago. Since that time, I doubt if that level of denial exists today; save for the NDE.

Joan

The conclusion of my research took a dramatic turn when Joan was diagnosed with advanced kidney cancer. She had not been feeling well for a few months but never complained. She ran a low-grade fever and had soreness in her legs. As a registered nurse with a high pain tolerance, and stubbornness to match, she would shun any suggestions to be examined. She chose self-diagnosis and insisted it was Lyme disease. She worked daily in the garden with our local deer population so that seemed like a probable diagnosis. To be sure she took part in a double blind two-month study with an experimental drug. At the end of the study there was no change in her condition; she was in the placebo group.

In the spring she accompanied me to a conference in Newport, Rhode Island; one of our favorite places. There were times when we would drive there just for lunch and, of course, the clam chowder. During the trip she was exceptionally lethargic and had difficulty walking. While helping her into the car I noticed that her ankles were swollen half again their size. After a brief discussion and stubbornness aside, we were packed and on our way home. She seemed relieved as her stubbornness didn't last very long and she slept most of the way home.

Our family physician saw her the next day and referred her to a urologist. Joan underwent several tests over the next two days and, after waiting anxiously, we were back in his office for the results. In as a professional manner as he could, he informed us that Joan had kidney cancer, which had spread to her lymph nodes and that one kidney was necrotic and not functioning. Joan glanced at me and squeezed my hand; we both had tears in our eyes. The doctor tried to provide some encouragement claiming that with aggressive surgery and chemotherapy there would be a 50/50 chance for survival. Being the fighter that she was she opted for all the treatments; she clung to the upper 50 percent. I provided what encouragement I could, not only for her but for me as well.

The surgery was very aggressive. The necrotic kidney was removed along with as many lymph nodes as possible without losing her on the operating table. I was told by the surgeon that not many people could survive an operation like that. If anyone could, Joan could. After a lengthy hospital stay, chemotherapy and experimental drugs, long hours were spent in the cancer treatment center. We watched movies, read books and did jigsaw puzzles. Once a week there was a group support session where everyone shared their progress or family stories. At the end of each session one person was assigned to tell a joke so that we could end on a happy note. It was difficult when one member would be missing and cancer claimed another victim.

Joan insisted on going back to work. She had since given up nursing administration and took a job as the nursing aide instructor at the local high school. She loved the job and the students loved her. The irony was that it was in the same school system as mine and fell under my jurisdiction. I recused myself from the hiring process but it still raised eyebrows. Little did they know that she was the real boss! She worked for about two months more until she no longer could and had to be helped out of the building.

Having a full-time administrative position, completing a thesis and caring for Joan was physically and emotionally draining. More than once I wanted to leave my studies and tend to her needs; she would not hear of it.

As if that were not enough, I was digging a hole for a fishpond in her garden when I developed a severe case of indigestion. It turned out to be a bit more than indigestion. I soon found myself in the hospital where I flunked a stress test. Not long after that I was on my way to emergency surgery at a major hospital for a quadruple heart by-pass operation. They wanted to air lift me there but the weather was too bad. That didn't bother me too much because I don't fly, but that's another story. Technically, riding in a helicopter is not flying. By definition, a helicopter is a bunch of airplane parts flying in relatively close formation.

As they were loading me into the ambulance, I told the doctor that I couldn't go and that I needed to take care of Joan. He looked at me with a grin and said, "If you don't go you won't be coming back to take care of anyone." Fortunately, our son was there for both of us. Interesting to note that I did not have an NDE during that operation.

Later on it became a question of who was taking care of whom. Were it not for the compassion and assistance of my university adviser Dr. Patricia Weibust the research would never have been completed. She was compassionate but kept me on task: stop your whining and write!

Joan's battle with cancer lasted for almost a year and a half with all the hopes, false hopes, encouragements and discouragements that go with it. I was able to administer the chemo injections at home, which allowed for fewer trips to the hospital. Aside from the pain of the injections the side effects were torturous. A feeling of extreme cold and violent shaking was followed by burning and profuse sweating. The shaking was so violent that it was necessary to hold on to her so that she wouldn't fall off the sofa or the bed and get hurt. There would be a brief respite. Then soon came more shaking and profuse sweating; cold compresses were needed to cool her down. The injections were given every other day for weeks. I wasn't sure if I was watching her get better or watching her die. She was a very strong-willed person and never complained.

In the evening, I would make dinner even though the most she could eat was a few mouthfuls and eventually just the smell of cooking made her lose her appetite. Everything tasted like metal, she said. I jokingly asked if my cooking was that bad. In the evening we would talk. Sometimes the discussion would center on things to do and look forward to when she was well. Other times she would talk about dying and not getting to do the things she wanted to do. I never knew which way the discussion was going to go. The important thing was to talk; she did not want to be alone. When she could, she would read: mostly books on dying and preparing for death. Later on I discovered Stephen Levine's book, *A year to Live*, in her belongings.

Joan

The weekends were around the clock caregiving so that our son could have a break. When she would take her afternoon nap, I would walk on the beach. It was cold and I was often the only one there. It was a good time to be alone and think. It was also a good time to cry. I thought of my NDE and what it was like for me but I wasn't ready to give her up to the experience; I wanted her with me for a long time; the experience can wait.

Joan loved the shore as much as I did. When she was up to it I would drive her one block to the beach where she would sit on a bench and stare out at the water. Her thoughts were revealed by the tears in her eyes and the anguish on her face. Was she thinking about my experience and what she learned from it? Was she afraid? Was she thinking about the death of our infant daughter Kathleen?

Eternity Revisited

Kathleen

Weep no more my child
The pain of birth is gone,
Fear no more my child
Life in brief has passed.

Rest in light, peace and warmth
With all that was and is,
No more in the angst of time
Beyond the needs of life.

In spirit you have become
One with all that be,
Love in its purest form
In eternity your soul is bathed.

Look down upon our lot
We, locked in time,
Mortal in all we do
Humble in our lack of sage.

Let your essence be our guide
That gift which you left behind,
Soon our turn will come
From the pain of birth and brief of life.
Weep not fear not anymore my child.

Joan

Why couldn't I make her more comfortable? That image remains with me to today. Occasionally I visit that bench; it will always be hers.

An unsympathetic employer made my caregiving difficult and compounded the issues. Putting in the required time at work was more important to them than taking time to care for Joan. Thirty-four years of service was not enough. One commented through the Human Services department (an oxymoron), that he didn't know it was going to go on forever. It made me think that if I hadn't got off the corporate ladder he might not have been where he was.

After her passing, the support that I expected from my own NDE was shockingly not there; my beliefs were shaken and questioned; I had met my second watershed. By all accounts I should have been happy for her: no more pain and suffering, just total peace and love. All that took a back seat to my selfish grief of loss. My lifelong friend and soul mate, my high school sweetheart had been taken from me. I would rather have her sick but here to take care of than not here at all. It was all about me. It was a stark reminder of being selfish and human.

Joan passed, with our children and me by her bedside in the hospital. She was heavily medicated but aware of our presence. I reminisced with her of the many good times we had, especially the humorous ones. The oncologist gave her two more weeks to live: she passed away that night. I told her I loved her one last time; she gave my hand a squeeze and she was gone.

Eternity Revisited

How it hurts when love is gone

And the words I love you cease to be,
No more touch or tender kiss
No warmth for me alone.

My needs are cast in loneliness
They float in lifeless void,
Never again to find the heart
That nourished them so long.

Life's blood now flows alone
No longer joined with hers,
Two that once were one
Are separate now forever.

No other love I seek
Nor life to take its place,
I leave all of what I am with her
For I have ceased to be.

Joan

> How it hurts when love is gone
> How lonely one can be,
> Now in sadness will I wander
> Away from all that was.

The next days were a blur with all the archaic customs of wake, funeral and reception planning. It wasn't all that difficult to plan as Joan had made her own funeral arrangements with her cousin who was a funeral director. The custom of viewing took place with an open casket. Four hours of staring at her lifeless body took its toll on my emotions as well as the parade of well meant, but grating, condolences. I kept my thoughts to myself as the parade passed:

"She's better off now."
She's not better off now, she's dead!
"She looks so good."
How can she look good? She's dead! She has too much makeup on and she's skin and bones.
"God only gives us what we can handle."
Excuse me ... is God in the business of punishing people?

"Life goes on."
You idiot, can't you see it's over?
"You'll get over it; try to keep yourself busy."
Must be related to the previous idiot.
"Hey, remember that great time when we ..."
No one will blame me if I hit him.
"It wasn't meant to be."
What wasn't, her to live or me to be happy?
"At least she isn't suffering anymore"
At least!

"She's in a better place."
Was there something wrong with where she was?
"It was her time."
Yeah? When's yours?
"Get on with your life."
Get on with your own life, better yet get one!
"Thank God you had her as long as you did."
Why? Was there a time limit?

They all meant well. They felt as though they had to say something, if not for me, for themselves. A simple I'm here for you or a hug is all that is needed.

It snowed on the day of her funeral and, despite school being canceled, many of her students attended. It was a beautiful service with eulogies. I don't recall much of what was said as I wept during most of it. Joan wanted to be cremated and her ashes planted with a tree. She wanted her death to give life. Her wish was granted on our property in Vermont.

Joan

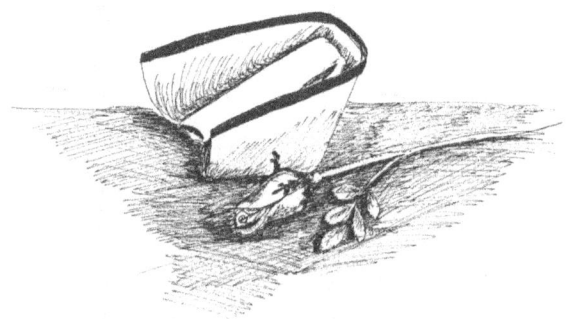

Joan

Her freshness flows
In scented rhythm
Gentle on my face.

Her tender touch
In pulsing warmth
Soft within my heart.

Her gracious form
In silent drift
Misty on my eyes.

Her impassioned sigh
In darkened whisper
Soft upon my ears.

Her love filled eyes
In eternal blue
Soothing to my mind.

Eternity Revisited

> Her peaceful presence
> In closeness transcends
> Lasting in my life.

I stopped sharing my NDE after Joan passed away, and fought off the emotions and knowledge that the experience had given me for so long. Although I stopped sharing, the experience continued to live in my mind through hidden thoughts that would bubble up to the surface unannounced. Those thoughts only occurred after my NDE and were written down on bits of paper in the middle of the night or on napkins during dinner. They made little sense and appeared to be the random firing of errant cerebral neurons during sleep. What makes them interesting is their subject matter of space and time. Perhaps one day they will make sense.

Doubt

Life began anew for the second time. The separation from one's high school sweetheart and abrupt change in daily life shook the very foundation of who I was. Consumed by the emotions of anger, denial, confusion and sorrow, logic and faith failed. I blamed the medical profession for not finding a cure for cancer and I still question the reason if there is one. I even resented her plants for living on without her and it would be a long time before I would move anything in the house from where she placed it. For the first time since my experience I questioned its validity, which was something that I thought would never happen. I shocked myself. It was unlike any prior death in the family and that includes our infant daughter, my mother, grandparents, aunts and uncles. I began questioning concepts that were made clear to me during my experience. The beauty of love and an unearthly existence was overshadowed by the immediacy of physical loss. It would be a while before the healing powers of time and a renewed interest in science and teaching would slowly close the wound, although the scar is still there. My experience was tested and, ironically as time passed, the very emotions I questioned were the emotions that healed. Love prevailed.

Recently one of my brothers passed away from cancer. He was a deacon in the Catholic church and was a religious and spiritual person. While I was visiting him in his final days, he confided in me that he was having doubts about death and what lies beyond. He felt guilty and quite upset. He reminded me of myself. My response to him was, "I seem to recall a very religious man, who was being crucified, having some doubts, and he was related to the boss!" He gave me a very warm smile. He passed a few days later. We had our issues growing up but we were always there for each other. Brotherly love is a very strong bond. It was another void created by the loss of a loved one; another part of me was gone.

Doubt

From my body flows my warmth

In stillness does it fade,
A darkness rest about my form
From shadow I am made.

A coolness fills my darkened heart
Where once a love held reign,
Now only echoes fill the void
Like the sound of distant rain.

In silent softness do I drift
As air becomes the ground,
A waning sun the only light
Evening's mist the only sound.

The past is gone
The present too,
The future I cannot see
I am no more of what I was
A part of me has ceased to be.

A Return to Teaching

During my grieving process for Joan, several projects were put on hold for lack of interest; writing and research became the major victims. I stopped writing poetry, and files of notes and monographs lay untouched. I functioned at work for two more years and retired. Retirement lasted less than a year when the thrill of being a dock bum and living on my boat began to wear thin. I began to feel intellectually barren and needed to fill a void. My thirst for knowledge was parched.

While I was staying on the boat my motivation to rejoin the planet came from an ironic source. A teacher friend of mine told me of another teacher whose twelve-year-old son was terminally ill with brain cancer and had but a few weeks to live. His last wish was to go fishing on a boat. She didn't even have to ask; "I'll take him!" I told her. She told me that he was in a wheelchair and very bloated from his medications. His movements were limited to his head and eyes; it would be difficult to get him on and off the boat. I had contacts with the fire department and the U.S. Coast Guard and when I explained what I was doing they were more than eager to help. I also enlisted my very large son to help.

The boy arrived at the dock by ambulance and the firefighters were waiting to carry him on the boat and put him in the fishing chair. There wasn't a dry eye on the dock. As a surprise, the Coast Guard was going to chase me on my way to the fishing grounds and board me. It wasn't long before the cutter pulled alongside with lights and siren going. The boy's eyes were as wide as they could be along with a struggled grin. Two of the men came on board and presented him with Coast Guard caps and pins and made him an honorary member. They stood at attention, saluted him and left, lights and siren going. I radioed them and thanked them. Their response was, "Captain, there isn't a dry eye on this boat."

"Nor here," was my response in a cracked voice.

The fishing was slow but, with my son helping him to hold the fishing pole, he was able to catch some fish. He radiated excitement that wasn't outwardly visible. His wish was granted and he slept all the way back to shore. The firemen were waiting and so was the ambulance. He died less than two weeks later. The message to me was clear: love prevails.

A few years prior to my retirement, I gave a lecture on the NDE at a local college. They called and asked if I would teach in the psychology department; one of the courses was Death and Dying, which was met with some apprehension. It turned out to be stimulating and rewarding, but, more importantly, I could feel life's juices begin to flow again; my NDE was once more the driving force. Students from two generations were in the same class, which made for a rich dialogue and sharing, each grounding the other in a common focus. The young matured and the elders found youth. I began to find myself once again. I didn't realize how much I had missed teaching. The second course on my schedule was Psych. 101; the only one in the room that enjoyed the course was me as the freshman did not expect another biology course. As it was an 8:00 a.m. class, most students perfected sleeping through it with their eyes open.

The death and dying course was not intended to be therapeutic: it was a course on various cultures and how they cope with death and the grieving process. It also helped them to reflect on their own concept of death and put it in the perspective of their own lives and the lives of their families. One assignment that I enjoyed giving was to have them write their own obituary. They found it very uncomfortable at first but soon became quite involved. The results were both interesting and, in some cases, humorous. It appeared that most of the females in the class saw themselves predeceased by their husbands. The males in the class primarily envisaged their demise as a result of a heroic event or feat. Almost all students saw themselves living to a ripe old age. One comical young man submitted the following obituary: John Doe passed away tragically on Tuesday. He was killed by a truck while jogging at the age of 109. One student wrote of her life ending by suicide; she was referred to a counselor. Some of the class discussions were emotional for some students. Not wanting them to leave upset, I required that at the end of each class someone was responsible for telling a joke. We all left laughing—a technique that I copied from the cancer support group.

The last chapter in the text addressed the near-death experience; a subject that would not have been mentioned thirty years ago. There was seldom a class that did not have a student who was in the process of losing someone or had recently lost someone. They were hoping for some comfort and guidance from the course in their quest for understanding. Many requested literature that would help them on a more personal level and something that they could identify with. Those requests and inquiries led to the self-publication of my book *The Four Moments after Death*. It was meant to be a supplement to the text. I used my experience of losing Joan to bring a relevancy to the course content and something they could identify with. I prefer to teach by example. It was my first attempt at writing a book and not a very good one. Some of it is incorporated in this book.

In contrast to teaching at the college, I was asked to teach a basic psychology course at a women's prison. It was an experiment to give inmates an opportunity to work toward a degree while incarcerated. I hesitated at first because I was once a person that put them there. Once I locked people up and I never got to see what their life was like after that; this was my chance to find out. I was old enough that they were much too young to be anyone I knew. That was fine until the warden introduced me as a former police officer. Fortunately, it made no difference to them; they were just happy to be able to have time away from their cells.

Being locked in a room with thirty women was a bit disconcerting. The officer in charge said he wouldn't be far away in case I needed him. He said there was a phone on the wall and if I needed help all I had to do was knock the receiver off the hook and help would come. When I arrived the following week for class, the phone had been ripped from the wall.

Most of the inmates were incarcerated for drug abuse or assault, and one for murder. There were women of all ages including middle-aged mothers with families. One young lady touched my heart. She was a very large young lady of color probably in her early twenties. She had an infectious smile and large happy eyes. It was hard to believe that she was incarcerated for assault. From the size of her I think I know who won. One day she told me, "I like you Dr. G. I promise I won't miss any of my anger management sessions." I responded that I would appreciate that very much.

During the course they all had a chance to share their life stories and motivations through written assignments. This was no easy task as every piece of paper and pencil had to be accounted for after class or there would be a lockdown, which included me. Staying overnight in a women's prison was not on my list of favorite things to do. It was sad to read so many accounts of abuse, despair and anger. They were all loving little infants at one time; what happened? There was obviously very little love in their lives now. I could see no evidence of an NDE in that class—then again maybe so. One thing they did have in common was a glimmer of hope, even the girl convicted of murder.

Another unique teaching experience was my being asked to teach the Disaster Psychology segment for the Community Emergency Response Team (CERT). In preparation I was given a two-inch-thick instruction manual for a one-day course! It was typical government issue with step-by-step instructions on what to say and how to say it. There was little room for discussion and no room for wandering from the manual. It would have been easier simply to give everyone a copy to take home to read. When it came time for class I used the manual as an outline and a paperweight. I filled in the blanks myself. I left the manual on a table in case anyone cared to look at it.

There were people in the class from many different occupations: nurses, teachers, business and industry, police and firemen. A one size fits all was not appropriate. Some in the class had experience dealing with trauma, mass casualties and death, while others had only read about it. All were allowed to share their experiences and the ways that they coped or did not cope. In an emergency these students were to take charge, treat, coordinate recovery efforts and provide emotional support. Their psychological preparation was important and, based on their individual backgrounds, the cookie cutter approach was inappropriate. Individual classes for individual groups would have been much more appropriate. A nurse or a veteran does not have the same training needs as a teacher. There is no boiler plate for dealing with trauma or death. There was a coordinator from CERT observing the class; I was not asked to come back.

Life Changes

Being without my soul mate for the first time since age 15 was overwhelmingly lonely. It was a long time before I moved anything around in the house. I left it the way she left it for fear of upsetting her. There were times at work when something would happen and I would pick up the phone to share it with her. The buzz tone became symbolic of my emptiness. In my mind she was still here but she was gone and there was no one at the other end of the line.

My search for companionship led to a few short-term social relationships and one more meaningful one, none of which worked out. I was told I was boring or depressing. My mother once told me that I wear my emotions on my sleeve; I guess she was right. I was looking for something that I was not going to find, something that no longer existed. Teaching and a return to poetry and old notes became my comfort level once more.

I was introduced by a cousin to a lovely lady from Newport. Ironically her name was Constance, the same name as my one sided, elementary school romance and my mother; interesting. No reference to Oedipus please. She was quite charming and our friendship did not take long to graduate into marriage. She was very sociable and dragged me kicking and screaming out of my social hibernation and injected me into the Newport social circle. She liked to travel, which forced me to experience being in new and faraway places. Included in the long list of things to catch up on was a refocus on the NDE and its impact on my life.

Looking back over the years since the experience, it is as vivid as if it were yesterday: none of it was lost. Its impact, however, has changed and consequently continues to change the course of my life. Immediately following the experience, I could no longer hunt; nor could I be a police officer again. Officers often have to make life or death decisions within seconds. Any hesitation can have dire consequences for all involved; I did not want to be put in that position again. Time has changed that to some extent. I still don't hunt but I enjoy taking my rifle for a walk in the woods in case something in the woods is hunting me. I'm sure that if my family or I were starving, all bets would be off and venison would be on the menu. I am too old to return to law enforcement but I do miss the opportunity to help and protect others, especially children, and to catch the bad guys. There is nothing in the NDE manual that says one can't be human again.

The years since my experience have not lessened my sensitivity to people or the importance of love in my life and empathy to those in need. Those same years have also not lessened my anger for social ignorance, selfish greed and hurtful people. I find myself extremely sensitive to issues that grate against everything, which the experience has left me with. The realms of political corruption, corporate greed, media bias and a morally questionable entertainment industry are glaring antitheses of the NDE. My yardstick is getting a workout. As time passes I see life's continuum bending downward and back onto itself in quantum fashion. Is it a pause in the evolutionary process? Or is it my perspective peering out from the NDE? I once said that I believe that love can be just as infectious as hate. That was in the eighties; today that is certainly being tested.

Among the changes experienced is, as noted previously, the re-emphasis of being, as well as doing. It has become easier in my senior years as arthritic knees prevent me from wandering too far. Being in a place of beauty and absorbing its essence with all the senses is an emotional osmosis, if you will.

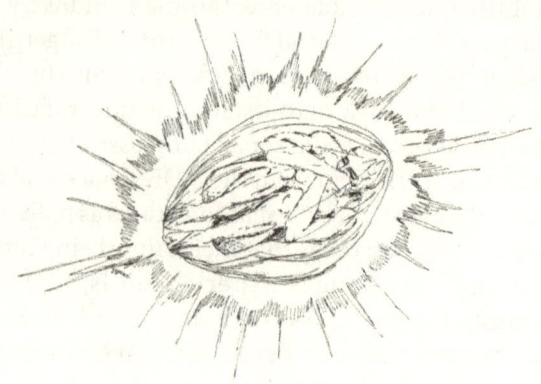

Within

I am unto myself
I peer out from within,
I capture all
That comes before.

I take my pleasures
Through my eyes,
I let them stir
And wake my mind.

They have free reign
Within my shell,
My heart and soul are theirs
My blood their stream.

That which lies within
Must remain,
Affect my walls or flee
It cannot.

Doubt

> For in rote
> My shell revolves,
> Routine hides my being
> Within is alone.

As a competitive sportsman I fished for trophies; today I fish for the experience and of course the food. The most important thing is being there: the smell of the ocean, the call of the birds, the touch of the breeze, and the splash of warm waters. Folks who must constantly be engaged in some kind of activity in such a place, miss most of what is there and most likely look upon the person who is *just being* as lazy or just plain no fun. I am still kicking and screaming at being dragged away. A trip to a local beach as seen through my eyes:

Eternity Revisited

Here we are at the public beach

My, what sights to see,
Miles of blankets, tons of flesh
And sand that can't be seen.

The smell of oils fills the breeze
And steals freshness from the air,
Gull and tern soar high and far
Returning not till beach is bare.

The jetty looks like Moby Dick
Harpooned and trying to sound,
With fishermen on its back
As poles and lines abound.

Even the tide is holding back
It isn't coming in,
It too must smell the ocean breeze
And fear the oils from human skin.

Doubt

It's dangerous at this public beach
As saucers spin and float,
And little people with pail and shovel
Happily dig their moats.

Lest all the senses be not forgot
That of sound has its abuse,
As metal spikes impale the sand
In search of musical ruse.

Each plays a different tune
Each competing with the next,
Together they create a din
That sends the brain in spasmodic wretch.

Ah now the sun begins to wane
These folks must fear the dark,
As off they slide on through the grass
To where their cars are parked.

As off they honk and stream away
The beach begins to breathe,
With gull and tern now at home
On the garbage feed.

The air is fresh as tide slips in
The sand is cooled by shadows long,
A stillness rests upon the shore
Moby Dick is gone.

I think I'll stay a minute more
As nature paints her sky,
And all I'll take from here
Is that which fills my eyes.

I greet travel with mixed emotions, for travel for the sake of travel, or just to brag that you have been here or there, holds no importance for me. To meet other people or learn other customs does have meaning. I suppose I have become an amateur ethnographer. We have so much to observe and learn in our own surroundings that one lifetime is not long enough to learn and appreciate it all. Perhaps it's our restless human nature that makes us always want to move and check to see if the grass is really greener on the other side of the fence. This itch to keep moving often takes us away from ourselves as well. Our lives have been so programmed to a fast pace, especially in our western culture, that even retirement may provide little respite. I wonder how I ever had time to go to work.

I experienced a great time of being when Joan and I celebrated our 25th wedding anniversary with another couple in the Virgin Islands. We chartered a boat and explored on our own. During our trip we anchored in an island harbor for an afternoon to check into customs. We ended up spending the night so we could attend the traditional island pig roast. On our return to the boat, a discussion took place on reports of pirates attacking tourists in the area. Everyone went below and locked themselves in their cabins for the night. Anchored off a Caribbean island, I was not to be denied a night under the stars. I slept on the bridge in my swim trunks, with a balmy breeze, awakened only by the island's resident rooster and rising sun. Blackbeard must have taken the night off.

The next anchorage was on an island not far away. Joan and the other couple took the inflatable dinghy into town to sightsee and shop. I did not come to the islands to shop. I chose to stay on board and read a book about

Doubt

the area's history with pirates. My junior high school English teacher would have been happy to see me read a book or, more importantly, to be on a boat somewhere else. It was exciting to look out at the very places the book was talking about. My imagination envisioned the incidents actually taking place. My absence from the onshore shopping excursion was obviously met with displeasure. It did have its reward, however, when another boat pulled up and anchored next to me. It was not the pirate ship I had envisioned; rather it was a ketch flying a French flag with an all female topless crew. Ah the rewards of solitude. When my crew returned they were greeted with a very broad grin.

A third incident on that trip was on another remote island—they were all remote—where I met a young boy on the beach. He was sitting by a wrecked dory half buried in the sand. He was eager to tell me about his very own boat and how proud he was of it. He did not see it as I saw it. His wishful thinking made it what he wanted it to be: a beautiful boat all his own. We chatted for a while and I was soon drawn into his vision of happiness. I began to see a bright, beautiful boat resting on the sand, waiting to take him on adventures at sea. He taught me a lot that day.

Eternity Revisited

In winter's stormy night

The summer's gale I feel,
In blowing drifts
On caps of white I sail.

The driven snow
Blows hard against my face,
Like ocean spray
As through the waves I race.

Toward the warmth of day
A respite from the cold,
Toward the light of spring
A respite from the old.

As a tree's barren bough
Adrift on moonlit snow,
My boom rests a port
In summer's starry glow.

The winter is my spring
The snow is my sea,
The cold is my warmth
The light is me.

As I Age

As one grows older, one becomes more acutely aware of time and the lack of it. As my father used to say, getting old is like having one foot in the grave and the other on a banana peel. His other favorite quote was, "life is like a roll of toilet paper: the closer to the end you get, the faster it goes." I thought it was funny until I was staring at my 80th year! What happened? Where did the years go? I'm just getting started and I'm near the end of the roll. Is it a coincidence that the tube at the end of the roll looks like a tunnel? Then it dawned on me: I was reborn after my NDE. I'm really only 44 years old. That works for my mind but someone neglected to let my body in on the secret.

Eternity Revisited

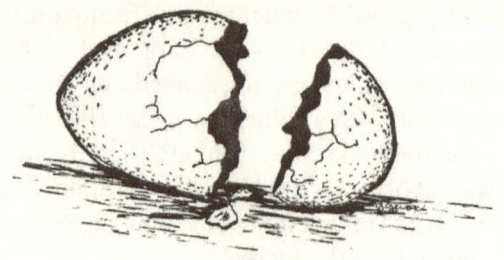

The Journey

Hidden in the innocence of my youth
My senior years lie in wait,
While hidden in my senior years
My youth beckons to return.

My journey through life
Is but a step toward who I am,
Years fall away laden with joys and sorrows
Only to show the peace and love of which I am made.

When my steps cease
And years are no more,
The essence of my being is born
Beyond my steps of flesh and time.

Look for me in your journey
I am with you though you cannot see,
I am guiding you though you cannot hear.
I lie deep within your heart and mind.

And when your journey ends
Leave to those which I have left to you,
Take what I have taken
Live on in the hearts and minds of those you have sown.

Doubt

I find that getting in touch with my mortality shifts my focus from reliance on external stimuli to an internal one. One indicator is my key chain. It used to hold keys to my boat, vacation home, lockers and other toys. Today it holds a house and car key. It is said that life is like a keychain, shedding what we don't need as we age. It is an introspection that magnifies my view of life and the world; I peer out from within. One of the interesting things about the NDE is that as beautiful as the experience is, it also emphasizes the importance of life. An eternity will always be there: this life won't; it is to be savored and enjoyed; there is no rush. Besides, I'm not done playing with my toys yet.

Then there is the insurance actuary who is trained to predict your life expectancy almost to the year. I wonder if the insurance companies are aware of the NDE. Living a long, healthy life is still a goal. During a lecture, someone once asked that if the experience was so great why don't you kill yourself and go back. Ignoring the poor sense of humor and sarcasm, I reminded him of the purpose of life and the taboo of suicide. Apparently, he was not paying attention.

One also becomes aware of time in day-to-day occurrences such as long-term projects. The older we get, the shorter the duration of long-term projects. A good example is having home renovations done later in life, as was the case with our home. Contractors are known for their delays; they are young energetic folks with a whole life ahead of them. Their concept of time differs significantly from that of the elderly and appears to be callously indifferent. A delay of weeks or months is nothing to them, but it is for people with limited years left. Who cares if the better roof has a twenty-year guarantee or the siding will last a lifetime?

Whose lifetime? Our contractor took almost a year to complete a two-month project: a year of living with friends, family and hotels. Not surprisingly, he went bankrupt soon after.

Going to the hardware or grocery store is also met with new vision. How many of these items do I really need? Do I really need the mega package of anything? Before Joan passed, she insisted that we go to the big box store to get enough things to get me through when she was gone. It was similar to preparing for a major snowstorm. She knew that she would not be needing them but I would. We made the most of the excursions and tried to make them fun. Joan was using a wheelchair at that point and was still learning how to steer it. On one occasion my steering went awry and we took out a freestanding display of greeting cards. It was good to hear her laugh but not so funny for the clerk.

As I continue to age, whether it has to do with the NDE or not, my thoughts have evolved from a self-centered daily routine mode to a more introspective one. My thoughts are of my existence in relation to my end: a long drawn-out life review, if you will. Having been trained to ask the right questions, I find myself questioning myself. My conscience won't allow me to judge or change my answers: it's brutally honest. Questions of life, love, family, work and contributions to those around me evoke both fond memories and some not so fond. I sometimes ask myself if I am growing older in my thoughts or am I growing younger? The two have much in common.

Doubt

Growing Young

How close they are
The young and old,
So simple in their needs
So fearful of the cold.

Wanting for care and love
Abandoned by their form,
Feelings locked within
Emotions quick to come.

Tender are their bodies
Nascent are their minds,
Void of all before
Each day new to find.

Care well for them
These very young,
For age belongs to time
Our time is yet to come

They're here for us to love
And protect them from the cold,
How close they are
The young and the old.

There is so much around us that can cure what ails us if we only stop long enough to let it. We tend to use and manipulate our surroundings rather than letting them do it to us. It makes one wonder how there could be crime and hatred on a beautiful tropical island. Some of the most beautiful places on Earth are rife with conflict. Why don't people don't let the elixir of beauty in and let it mold them?

Doubt

The Islands

A beauty rests upon these isles
Silent in peaceful hues,
A beauty painted in shades of life
Pastels of ships and crews.

A beauty rests upon these isles
Found deep in hearts and minds,
A beauty that grows and spreads its wings
Alight on faith and joy to find.

As mangroves spread their roots of life
For generations yet to be,
So islanders spread their love
Spawned from earth and sea.

Here time has no place
Nor are shadows cast,
For light abounds in all that's seen
And what lies hidden in isle's ancient past.

Eternity Revisited

What you see is not of Earth
But the souls of those who live,
Love is what rules this realm
A single pulse of those who give.

Routine will not be found
Haste will have no place,
Ease is all you'll find
Nature in all her grace.

Post-NDE Views of Life

Since my NDE it is obvious to me that my paradigm of life has gone through a metamorphosis. My views of life have evolved, based on my life experiences; all are based on that day in 1977. My opinions, behavior and doubts are rooted in the knowledge and emotion of that near-death experience. A strong sense of what is right and what is wrong governs my actions. In expressing my thoughts, I am unable to separate them from the love and perfection of that eternity; they are either in concert with them or in conflict with them. Unfortunately, in my later years, I have found worldly events to be mostly in conflict with them. I reflect on subjects that have impacted my attention because of the experience:

Media

As I said earlier, I believe that love can be just as infectious as hate. It was not long after my experience that I was filled with euphoric love and hope. I still hold that love, and hang on to hope; the euphoria, however, has dimmed. Global changes during the last few decades have seemed to emphasize the infection of hate, a term I refused to recognize, believing there is either love or the absence of it. I say *seemed* because we are informed of happenings by the media and they determine what we should know and how we should think. Very few people control the information, which the masses get. Each media source has its own political and philosophical narrative, which negates true unbiased reporting. People tend to view or read the source that most agrees with their own political and philosophical beliefs; hence they feed off each other. It is little comfort for people looking for peace and harmony in their life.

Negativity sells, and, on the daily news and in newspapers, that's pretty much what we hear and see and read. A steady diet of it paints a grim picture of the global state of affairs; positive news is largely ignored.

Reflected in our society's fascination with sports, as in car racing for example, is as I suspect, not the thrill of the race but of the impending crashes. Football is not far behind with violent body contact and videos of the ten hardest hits of the week. It's incredible that we prepare young children for a violent sport through midget football. Their little bodies are still forming and are being abused. I believe that parents and coaches are often living out their fantasies through their children for reasons only known to themselves, but most likely because they want their children to achieve what they didn't manage. Their tantrums during the games attest to that. But, again, I digress. It's interesting how people from both teams pray to God for a win. Do they really believe that God has skin in the game? Praying that no one gets hurt would be a better wish.

We are not far removed from the events of the Roman Coliseum and its elaborate spectacle of human pain and suffering for the pleasure of the disassociated masses. The most recent spectacles are in the form of reality shows where viewers can project themselves into situations that they could never perform themselves, similar to midget football. Yet they have the privilege to criticize and judge others from the comfort of their easy chair. It is a sad indictment of society.

Our evolution includes more efficient ways to kill each other. Apparently, violence is in the DNA of most creatures to satisfy hunger, sex, possession and dominance: all biological traits. The NDE has none of that. It would be interesting, once DNA is completely mapped, if that gene could be removed. I wonder if ET has accomplished that. A world without violence? That would be as close to an NDE as we will get on this planet. I once commented in an interview that one way to save humanity is for everyone to have an NDE. That didn't go over very well.

I also wonder what would happen if only good news was emphasized? Would bad news slowly dissipate in time from the forefront of consciousness? Emphasis on good could become catchy. The same goes for the entertainment industry.

"How far that little candle throws his beam! So shines a good deed in a naughty world." Shakespeare: *The Merchant of Venice.*

The entertainment industry has its own powerful influence on society. It provides for many informative and educational venues that promote a positive global awareness and it brings us to places that we would probably never see or experience. The plight of species and the changing climate are brought into our homes.

The flip side of the coin is that it also successfully capitalizes on human emotions and senses and often finds new ways to manipulate them. Whether it's TV, movies, video games or cartoons, they desensitize the viewer into a numbing addiction. Violence and sex are their most successful moneymakers. Violence has always been part of human behavior; it has simply been improved to include most aspects of life and provide a manual for commission. The person looking for peace and harmony in their life will have to search deep in the entertainment industry.

Sex is also a best seller and, when combined with violence, it provides its own entertainment. Freud's theory that much of human behavior is sexually motivated is hard to dispute, despite his addressing the suppression of sex during the late Victorian era. Freud has been maligned for some of his theories and methods. Someone please show me how modern day entertainment is not sexually based or motivated. Imagine taking all human sexual content or visuals out of a movie: what would be left? Most likely will be a nature documentary or a cooking show. Sexual exploits are not new: check the depictions on the walls of Roman brothels, Egyptian paintings or Kama Sutra. The difference from today is that back then they were limited to their own venues. Today it is difficult to find a place not under sexual influence; it permeates most aspects of society and age groups. One must admit that the content only exists because it is heavily supported by enough people to make it profitable.

In defense of the Hollywood actors, it is acknowledged that they have agents whose sole job is to keep them in the news and make money. I'm sure that they are coached on what to say or do, making them pseudo experts on everything from food to politics. I am reminded of the definition of an expert someone once shared with me: An expert is one who owns a briefcase and lives more than a thousand miles away. The term itself is broken down; thus, X is an algebraic expression, which unless given a value means nothing. A spurt is a drip under pressure. I am also sure that some of their personal lives are not as bizarre as they purport to be in public; I hope.

From adolescence on, the sex drive is natural and necessary to procreate the human race, or, as Campbell put it, "life is a lot of protoplasm with an urge to reproduce and continue in being". Hollywood has managed to pervert a natural instinct.

Fortunately, as we get older, the reproductive drive wanes, in most of us, and so does the preoccupation. We are free to enjoy other preoccupations and motivations from procreation to pro-reflection, such as writing a book. If we balk too long at the aging process, our bodies will remind us whether we like it or not. The brain is slower to adapt. Young thoughts in an old body can be disappointing and troublesome. The mirror was once my friend; not so much now. It is, however, an emotionally grounding instrument.

A growing concern is that of the UFO phenomenon. If anything has the potential for getting global attention, this would be it. It may be something to fear, then again perhaps not. I suspect that it won't be long before we find out if it is a phenomenon or not. It may better fit my definition of an unexplained reality.

Believing in the UFO phenomenon is not necessarily in conflict with religion or the NDE. A belief in a God of creation is not limited to Earth. Of all the billions of stars and planets, it is inconceivable that Earth is the only planet with intelligent life, and I use that term loosely. Whether or not they have visited or are already here is open to conjecture. There is an alleged body of evidence that suggests, perhaps, they are here or at least have been here. If they have visited or observed us, it was most likely for entertainment. If they want to watch drama or violence, tune in to Earth. If they wanted to watch comic relief, tune in to Earth and watch them try to explore space with the equivalent of bottle rockets. It is interesting to note that while alleged UFOs zip around at incredible speeds under tremendous G forces, dip in and out of water with no visible means of propulsion and in total silence, we are selling seats on space rides.

I have met some people who, I'm convinced, missed the ship for their ride home. They were probably intentionally left behind for us to deal with.

The realm of science fiction, or maybe not; the various life forms on Earth may have evolved somewhere else and made Earth their home. The myriad of species and their environments make it difficult to believe they evolved from each other on Earth. Could it be that each has a home planet somewhere? If such is the case, we may want to think twice about contacting them. They may not be very happy about how we treated their ancestors. Science fiction? Many of the UFO sightings have been around nuclear facilities or vessels. Could it be that they have developed beyond organic food for their subsistence and rely on nuclear energy for food and power, or are they worried that we are in danger of destroying the planet? My apologies; my thirst for knowledge sometimes runs away with me. There are, however, many things that were once considered science fiction, which are now reality: the Dick Tracy wrist-phone, for example, for you older folks.

The popularity of the "Ancient Astronauts" TV series attests to the growing interest and belief in the extraterrestrial phenomenon. Researchers suggest that the similarities in structures and stories of creation throughout time on the planet are the result of extraterrestrial visitors. Some academics, such as Campbell, posit a hypothesis that the common psyche innate in all mankind transfers to all cultures. The NDE can accommodate both schools of thought.

One of my science lectures to my Jr. high school science class attempted to explain life on Earth in relation to the cosmos. On the chalkboard—smart boards were not invented yet—I put a tiny speck of chalk. I then drew the solar system so that they could barely see it. The spiral galaxy was next. Four and a half inches from that was the nearest star, Alpha Centauri. A definition of a light year followed: the distance that light travels in one year at 186,000 miles per second. Our nearest star is four-and-one-half light years away. Now that I had their attention, I filled in the entire board and around the room with other galaxies and stars until I told them that I ran out of room to put them all up; we would probably need all the chalkboards in the whole school and then some. When I finished I asked them if they thought we were alone.

The next day the principal called me into his office; I've been to the principal's office as a student but never as a teacher. He had received complaints from some parents that their children were unable to sleep. Compounding the problem was that these were some of the same parents who complained when I dissected a chicken in biology class, resulting in their parents having to take chicken off their dinner menu.

The use of the microscope was once met with awe. It opened up a whole new previously unseen world. People were amazed at the life teeming in a drop of pond water. They were also in horror when examining the scrapings from under their fingernails. Back to the principal's office! It did cure many from biting their nails. Students are very impressionable at that age and I took advantage of it to help them to learn. I abandoned some demonstrations for fear of having parents march on my house with torches and pitchforks. Jr. high school was more than making a volcano or sticking pins in butterflies: it was fun.

Belief in the extraterrestrial phenomenon is not in conflict with the NDE for many of the same reasons as for religion. The NDE is not earthly: it is beyond that. Anything not of earth will easily fit into the NDE discussion.

Soon after publicly sharing my experience, I was asked by a popular actress if I believed in reincarnation. My response was that I couldn't comment on it one way or the other because I haven't thought about it. It was not one of the topics I gleaned from the experience. Since then I have given it some thought.

Given that many things we don't currently understand are possible, why shouldn't reincarnation be a possibility? Many religions and cultures are firm believers in reincarnation. Accounts of *déjà vu* are attributed to the phenomenon. Is it possible that during their NDE, when experiencers were told to go back, it was not necessarily as themselves? Could a man return as a woman? A woman as a man? That could explain some behavioral anomalies. If that is the case, there is a whole lot of reincarnation going on. In the realm of different levels of consciousness, is it possible to go dimension hopping? Transgender may be thought a fad for some but not for others. The concept of reincarnation deserves objective thought beyond our prejudices and learned limitations.

Philosophy, Pseudoscience and Science

Pseudoscience in ancient times was considered a science and a scholarly study. Astrology was revered in many cultures. It has been mentioned in many documents and works, including those of Shakespeare and Chaucer. In more recent times, it has fallen from grace thanks to the development of the scientific method. In the prediction of behavior and events by the alignment of stars and planets, astrology was unable to stand up to the test of scientific validity and was banished to the realm of pseudoscience.

Paranormal events have also failed to earn a place at the scientific table. It is, however, being given increased attention. Aside from making good fodder for Hollywood horror films with nasty ghosts, not all paranormal events can be explained. One unexplained event occurred in our own home. It was a large, old, Victorian style house set back from the road on a hill; it could pass for the Bates hotel. I liked the old style but our teenage children did not. They thought it was haunted and there was a time when I thought it might be also. I did some research on the previous owners and learned that their older son had committed suicide by hanging himself in the wine cellar. I was a bit taken back because my daughter refused to go into the wine cellar from day one; she said it gave her the creeps. When I told the family the story, I changed the place of the hanging to the attic. It wasn't until after we moved, years later, that I told her the truth.

A second event was finding footprints embedded in the carpet in the bedroom, which neither we, nor professional cleaners, could get out. There are, allegedly, good ghosts/spirits as well like Casper the friendly ghost. We didn't get to meet him.

Psychics are also without a seat at the science table. Psychics claim to be able to predict your future and put you in touch with deceased friends or relatives via a seance, and a crystal ball; all for a modest price of course. The crystal ball dates back to the Druids and has a role in several cultures and religions throughout the world. It was originally believed that it was a cure for anything from disease to bad karma. Only since recently has it been used to summon up spirits of the dead in a rather carnival atmosphere and setting. It may provide emotional comfort to some but it is a long way from being considered a science.

It is unfortunate that the legitimate aspect of pseudoscience, in general, is overshadowed by individuals using it purely for profit and attention. The same is true for any phenomenon: I suspect the NDE as well. The number of people believing in and following pseudoscience attests to its relevance to a substantial population. It deserves the same scrutiny as the NDE, which some also refer to as pseudoscience. However, extensive research has propelled the NDE to the status of a viable phenomenon. With more understanding of physics and research on consciousness, materialist science is on shaky ground.

How does the NDE fit into all of this? Despite the efforts of some, the NDE is not in the entertainment business. NDErs are not actors or in the business of convincing people of what they know. Most do not have daily updates on their knowledge. I succumbed to two requests to reenact the NDE for TV. One was to be put on a gurney and wheeled into the emergency room and the other to walk on the beach while staring out to the sea. I felt totally uncomfortable and ridiculous doing both. I would never make it in Hollywood. Lying on the gurney faking near death was easy: I just had to lie there with my eyes closed. Walking on the beach, I had difficulty coordinating my leg and arm movements as if I never walked before. Many NDErs speak of relatives or friends whom they encountered during their experience. They do not, however, hang a sign outside their home advertising "50% off today to visit your deceased relatives". For a fee of course.

Astrology appears to be limited to planets and stars in our own solar system and galaxy but what of the rest of the universe? Do other solar systems and galaxies have their own astrological forecasts? The NDE is clearly of the cosmos as has been depicted numerous times in the experiences.

More often than not, pseudoscience deals with foreboding omens and frightening images. The power of suggestion plays a major role in its belief system as well as a self-fulfilling prophesy. If one surrounds oneself with enough negativity some of it is bound to rub off. The NDE is totally positive, save for a few accounts of negative ones, which I personally cannot come to terms with and question them as being NDEs. That is not a very popular statement but it belongs to me. As I stated on the Donahue Show, the God I have come to know is incapable of anything but love. Before I'm thrown into the naysayers lair, I am in defense of pseudoscience in that it falls under the same category of anything is possible and deserves to be listened to and be subjected to serious research.

Naysayers

As with any phenomenon or -ism, there is a force or psyche whose purpose it is to critique or disprove it. The NDE is no exception. It wasn't long after the phenomenon came out of the closet that there were those who tried to push it back in. The NDE got the attention of medical and psychological communities and, while some acknowledged the profound implications of the experience, others attempted to define it in strict materialist science terms.

In 1996, the New York Academy of Science published a series of papers in a volume titled "The Flight from Science and Reason." It could be considered the naysayer's bible. It takes to task every institution and belief system that does not meet empirical scientific proof from health and environment to religion and education.

In one of the essays by skeptic, Paul Kurtz, he lumped astrology, the NDE and reincarnation into the paranormal. He claimed that the fact that NDErs report similar accounts, regardless of location on the planet, is due to humans sharing a common physical and psychological structure. Is he using a phenomenon to debunk a phenomenon? He went on to lament the fact that there were so few critics of the NDE, which caused it to gain in popularity. Perhaps it is because many of the proponents of the NDE are from his scientific community: some having experienced it themselves. He ended his argument by stating that the brain goes through a dying process and ones who survive have life-altering values and priorities due to their harrowing brush with death, harrowing? He attributed the dying brain process as the most likely cause of altered states of consciousness.

Kurtz's critique of reincarnation, strangely enough, was not as critical as that of the NDE. His explanations referred to its history and role in other cultures. With tongue in cheek, I pose the following question: Could the NDE be considered a form of reincarnation? NDErs have experienced death and returned. In many cases they are not the same person. There are reports of divorce because of it, change in lifestyle, knowledge, values, etc. They report a feeling of being reborn and seeing the same things for the first time.

Other explanations include the effects of drugs and medications. During my recovery I was on medication and I did have a dream, which seemed real but did not come close to my near-death experience.

In my dream I was walking up a grass covered hill toward a small stone church at the top. There was no surrounding scenery, just a light mist. The church had a doorway but no doors; it had windows but no glass. The inside was gray and bare; it looked cold but it was warm. There was no furniture except for a small stone altar in the center. On the altar was an infant with a young woman standing next to it. I approached the infant and looked; it was I.

Greek philosophers are credited with the beginning of philosophy and science circa 625 B.C. In reading the accounts of Socrates and Plato, one may wonder where their knowledge came from. Their inquiries into the cosmos were not unlike our inquiries today and not unlike most NDE accounts. The early scholars were in search of the nature of reality as we are today. They philosophized not only about matter but also about the roles that values, virtue and logic play. Socrates believed that the first step to gaining knowledge was to acknowledge one's ignorance; sound familiar? Also familiar is that the writings of the early philosophers had a healthy dose of humor: a bit dry but humorous.

Plato believed in two separate worlds: one materialistic, the world of the senses, and the other of the mind, soul and reason. He believed that the world of humans might cease to exist but the super-sensory world of ideas continues. He further believed that men are not born equal but that they have different amounts of good, bad and reason at birth: the balance of good and bad being determined by reason, which determines the continued existence of the soul.

Quite profoundly the "Doctrine of Recollection" states:

> Since true knowledge cannot be acquired through the senses, all learning and knowledge is recollection by the divine, immortal soul of knowledge, which it possessed before it entered the body.

NDErs speak of total knowledge during the experience but don't recall it when they return to their senses.

Unfortunately, religious zealots have long stymied the advance of science. Ignorance in the guise of heresy retarded the evolution of man's knowledge. The Dark Ages, Spanish Inquisition and even the Salem witch trials attest to the theories of early religion. Today is no exception to evolutionary naysayers.

The NDEr does not necessarily dismiss some of the scientific explanations of the experience, since changes obviously occur physically to the body, in particular the brain, at the time of the event. None of the materialist science explanations, however, explain the post-physical and un-earthly accounts beyond the moment of death and during the clinically dead time period. Nor do they explain the out-of-body experience where people have been able to give a detailed account of all that went on around them while they were clinically dead. Out-of-body experiences might attest to the non-biological aspect of the NDE. If people can see themselves on a stretcher or read instruments while clinically dead, what are they seeing? Their eyes are down there in their body.

The NDE can be explained in medical and psychological terms only up to the time of death: after that, no earthly theories or definitions apply. The refusal to call the experience anything but "near" conveniently cuts off the debate of anything beyond it and leaves it strictly in the realm of established scientific principles, hence my frustration with the term.

As part of my own research, I plotted my subjects responses to pre and post NDE attitudes and behavior. I used an adaptation of the Torus model, which I affectionately call the doughnut. It was the same model used by philosopher and inventor Arthur M. Young in his "Theory of Evolutionary Process." His theory was an early attempt to combine science, math, and philosophy as a way to restructure scientific thought, which would include both spiritual and physical dimensions. His theory also connects science and consciousness through quantum physics, which he refers to as the light and spiritual core of existence.

I chose the Torus model because of its similarities to the NDE and its aftereffects. On the surface of the Torus I plotted intensity of each respondent's current values, attitudes and behaviors. The center (doughnut hole) represents the NDE. Emerging on the other side of the Torus are the changed levels of values, attitudes and behaviors at a higher level of consciousness. One may liken the center to a black hole where gravity, so dense, does not allow light to escape. In essence it is not black at all but an extreme concentration of light, (a beautiful bright loving light at the end of a dark vortex).

It would be interesting for future researchers to continue to connect the dots of the physical and behavioral sciences. Finding a common denominator is a challenge but possible. It is my opinion that the NDE will play a significant role, if not be the answer. A definitive link between the physical and metaphysical would do Parmenides proud. When that link is defined, I'm sure the next debate will be that the NDE is simply another level of consciousness. My response would be, don't let logic cloud your thinking.

The NDE has been experienced by people of all faiths and atheists around the globe, and perhaps one of the issues causing confusion surrounding the NDE is that despite accounts of God, peace, love etc., for most NDErs it is not a religious experience but a spiritual one.

We are reminded that most NDErs are not interested in convincing anyone about the validity of the NDE or in preaching its merits; it is not a religion or a cult.

Philosophy, Pseudoscience and Science

They seldom bring the subject up on their own for discussion and are comfortable with the opinion of others. Their experience is conveyed by their radiance. It is not appropriate for a cocktail party discussion as I painfully found out on a few occasions. If people believe in the experience, fine; if not, that's fine also. To judge others or force one's belief upon others goes against what the experience is about and has little to do with the scheme of things. By and large, the NDErs response to the naysayers is not in the form of a debate but in rather simple questions.

If a segment of the scientific community claims to have debunked the NDE for lack of proof or empirical evidence, are they not stifling the ever-expanding parameters of science? Are not the recent discoveries in quantum physics, nanoscience, Higgs Boson (the 'God particle') and Hubble images enough reason to investigate the continued function of the mind verses the limited physical function of the brain? Why do people who have had an NDE maintain the alleged endorphin-induced euphoria for the rest of their lives, long after the original stimulus is gone? If the NDE is a result of the body's preparation for death then why is it that not all people who have been clinically dead and revived have the experience? Lastly, is it possible for humans to have a spiritual DNA that lives on in memories and actions when one is no longer alive? I encourage the scientific community to pursue their efforts in accepting or falsifying the NDE. Without wanting to repeat myself, I believe I know what awaits them.

One time I visited Rome and toured the Coliseum and the Pantheon. While at those sites I could not help but feel thrown back to that era. The people and the sounds of then were as much a part of the experience as the visuals. The cheers, pain and suffering were also there. It was certainly an emotional and empathetic experience brought on by previous knowledge of their history but why? The same feelings came over me at Stonehenge. I had goose bumps as I walked around it and let my mind run with the hidden history. It also came alive in my mind. Could there be a spiritual DNA hidden in the dark matter of our molecular structure? Are we not beginning to understand that space is not really space but, rather, a different type of matter?

As we expand our knowledge of time, space, and consciousness we are finding similarities to the description of the NDE. A sense of timelessness and knowledge far beyond our Earthly limitations.

It has been accepted that man continues to evolve, both physically and intellectually. Why then do we set limits on our abilities and our horizons? Are we not retarding our own evolution? All one has to do is to look back at history and the discoveries that were made with daring and vision, which challenged established thought, principles and fears, including accounts of death experiences in antiquity. Ignorance is not reserved for the uneducated: the intellectual has a right to it also. The most intelligent thing a person can do is to acknowledge their own ignorance, in the manner of Plato, and understand that ignorance prevents one from going beyond it. Man is rather arrogant in boasting of his evolution in life and intelligence in the brief time he has been in existence. By comparison he has progressed but a nanosecond from a Neanderthal. Our knowledge is astronomically fragmented as evidenced by Earth's fragmented societies.

The strong residual effect of the NDE is that many things, which we are unaware of, are possible in the

Philosophy, Pseudoscience and Science

total knowledge of the experience. While we are alive we have abilities far beyond what we believe we have. These abilities and potential knowledge have the power to create a behavior altering global peace and freedom from disease and hunger. It is Utopian and stands in stark contrast to current world events where greed and ignorance seem to rule. We spend more money on eye makeup than eye research.

Earth is in its infancy compared with other worlds and we have a long way to go before we can boast of a unified global civilization where all cultures share in a common good for the benefit of this planet and beyond. The gaps in such a unification currently paint a mosaic of a young and disconnected civilization made up of different species running around bumping into each other.

It would be interesting to see if man's evolution leads in that direction or is destined to collapse upon itself in nova fashion, creating an end to the evolutionary cycle rather than a continuum. As someone who has experienced something beyond here, I believe that the continuum is possible.

We already know that planets, stars and solar systems have limits to their existence. Man need not end with his planet. It would be a shame if a well-placed meteor wiped out any evidence of man. He has the potential intelligence to continue beyond this planet if he so chooses. Those who are critical of space exploration do so for a myriad of reasons. They may be financial, social, political, fear or simply a severe lack of intellect. One who keeps one's head embedded in the crust of the Earth exposes an unpleasant part of their anatomy for all to see and communicate with.

I continue to struggle in my attempt to convey my experience of death. My thoughts and comments vacillate between the physical and metaphysical and, admittedly, are difficult to follow; then again that gap between the two is the unexplained reality of the NDE, which has yet to be fully understood. If anything can be learned from the NDE by those who have not had the experience, it is the importance and beauty of life and the tool of love to live it despite trials. Using the accounts of the NDE as an excuse to escape life and its trials is not what it is about. Tapping into nature in our tiny little world is the elixir.

Losing sight of that was clearly evident during the pandemic. Being quarantined and having few places to go was traumatic for many people. People who relied on external stimuli to make them function were most at risk. Those least at risk were those who were able to internalize their life and refocus on the important little things in their life. Instead of requiring attention from others, some found time to pay attention to themselves. We can live without a trip to the mall or a cocktail party. Then again if you are a practicing hermit or just plain anti-social you are probably asking yourself, "what pandemic? What did people do before the technology explosion?" Having reached 80 I can tell you. We read, we wrote and we conversed.

The NDE message, as I said in the beginning, is to live one's life with an emphasis on love and less emphasis on window dressing. Perhaps the reason that not everyone has an NDE, when they clinically die or come close to death, is that some were sent back to get the message out. Hello up there, we can use some more help down here!

I firmly believe that the lessons and knowledge learned from the NDE can be the vehicle by which universal harmony can exist and all are absorbed in the love, peace and knowledge of its light. This visit to eternity has been brief in time but timeless in our ultimate level of consciousness.

Eternity Revisited

Philosophy, Pseudoscience and Science

Metamorphosis

Born of shadows cast from years before
Wrenched from light, peace and love,
Born to the pain of breath, touch and thought
Born to a world of fear and anger.

Now wrapped in time I'm ushered along
Older in each hour,
On its own my life passes by
A quilt of joys, sorrow, life and death.

In the wane of light I now reflect
Upon the innocence and brashness of youth,
Immersed in a search for things unreal
Caught in the tide of human needs.

Now in my ebb wisdom flows
Waking from its long deep sleep,
With values new and lessons learned
Ignorance and vanity erode away.

Thoughts now trek back through time
The journey provides a familiar path,
Unlike the first I do stumble
In reverie I float above the roots.

A cycle not yet complete
From blind cocoon to endless flight,
Tired wings now seek to rest
From youthful stance to humbled frame.

Soon to return to a place that once was
My journey brief yet long in time,
Back to the light that gave me life
Back to where I have always been.

Acknowledgments

If it were not for Ken Ring I don't know if or when I would ever have shared my experience. It has been through him that I was able to meet many wonderful people whose acceptance and understanding gave my life new meaning. From that first day in his office to the Near-Death Hotel (Ken's home) to the many interviews and appearances, he will always be a very dear friend.

One of the first people Ken introduced me to was Bruce Greyson. The bond with Bruce was immediate, not only to me but my family as well. Bruce became my friend on many levels: support, a mentor and doctoral adviser. This book would not have been possible were it not for his encouragement and advice.

Pat Weibust, my university professor and doctoral adviser, guided me through my research and through Joan's illness and death. It is difficult to find the words of how much Pat's understanding and compassion meant to me and still does. When I wanted to quit my research to take care of Joan she wouldn't hear of it; that "we can do it" attitude still echoes. Her visits to Joan helped more than one can imagine.

Despite the fact that my parents never finished high school, they knew the importance of having an education. My mother was self-taught and quite articulate both as a member of the board of education and a patron of the arts. Her kind, nonjudgmental encouragement played a major role in my early education. She always found time for all five of her sons.

My father was from the school of tough love. Showing weakness was for losers and sissies. His encouragement was in the form of ridicule if I failed; I was an embarrassment to him. It wasn't until my fifties or sixties that I felt a hug or heard the words "I love you" and understood that he was proud of my educational accomplishments. I can't fault him for that; it was the way he was raised and treated by his father. I know he loved me and that's all that matters.

To P.M.H. Atwater, many thanks for sharing some of the subjects from her own research for my study. It was an unselfish giving that was most appreciated.

Lea Newsome, whose gift of Joseph Campbell's *The Power of Myth*, which was an inspiration for segments of the book.

I am most appreciative of the subjects of my research who so unselfishly shared their experiences for my study and contributed to the meaning of the NDE.

Although I do not know his name, the young boy on the beach in the Virgin Islands will not be forgotten nor his vision of what life is if we look hard enough.

Sometimes a person can encourage you in a negative way. For that I am grateful to my one professor who had an obvious disdain for former police officers. I appreciate his unsuccessful attempt to undermine my program. He reminded me that in one's attempt to reach a goal, there will be roadblocks, which must be

Acknowledgments

faced and dealt with. He strengthened my resolve and faith in my purpose. Thank you.

The reality of my NDE has brought with it a *knowing* that friends and family who have passed are part of it, just they are part of the writing of this book. Each contributes the best of themselves to make me who I am. My grandparents, parents, wife, and infant daughter continue to live on in my consciousness and guide me through my life with their love. This book is also about them.

My late brother, Gerald, whose sketches illustrating my poetry will live on along with my love for him.

Jon Beecher whose guidance and patience has made this book a reality. His confidence in me and the experience helped me to fulfill one of my life goals.

I have stressed many times in this text the importance of young children and the NDE; obviously I can't say it enough. During the writing of this book, the news has been filled with numerous accounts of child abuse and death. It has pained me to control my anger at the inhumanity. I plead that their pain and suffering not be in vain, and that their plight gets the attention it deserves. If anyone reads this book, I would hope it would be from the Nobel foundation and accept my challenge to award the peace prize to an infant. Maybe then people will start to get the message. For little AJ from all of us:

Eternity Revisited

We Did Nothing

While little AJ was tortured and beaten in a cold shower
We watched it on the news,
And did nothing.

While little AJ slowly died in pain
We watched a movie,
And did nothing.

While little AJ's parents consumed drugs
We read it in the paper,
And did nothing.

While drug dealers sold drugs
We protested,
And did nothing.

While politicians gave lip service to drug abuse
We complained,
And did nothing.

While we lay in a warm bed
Little AJ lay wrapped in plastic on the cold ground,
And we did nothing.

As we went about our day
Little AJ's life of five years came to an end,
And we did nothing.

How many more AJs are out there?
Crying alone,
while we do nothing.
How many of us are accomplices to his death
When we do nothing?

Epilogue

I had my students write their own obituary; it is only fair that I submit my own; poetically of course.

I Told You So

Damn this poetry
That no one seems to want.
At least for now
Perhaps when I'm long forgot.

I remember my college days
Picking Chaucer's brain.
Elliot, Stevens and Poe
All that search in vain.

They were not of now
Nor here nor then,
They were of tomorrow
A place we've not been.

Eternity Revisited

How foolish are you all
Who look at yesterday,
What a waste of now
What a price to pay.

Life continues on
It never turns around,
All that comes to pass
Will never go beyond.

If one could take the past
And bring it back to them,
Then no one would have died
There would be no again.

All would be now
Stagnant in its being,
We would not learn of them
Nor of how to be.

Leave all for tomorrow
Do not hold the past,
Let today be but a moment
It's time that makes one last.

A day will come when time is not
And all that is lost,
No sound, touch or sense
Nothing but a thought.

Listen to my words
And all that I have said,
How foolish you all were
To wait till I was dead.

References

Atwater, P.M.H. (1996). Children and the Near-Death Phenomenon: Another Viewpoint. *Journal of Near-Death Studies.* 15. (1), 5-15.

Campbell, J. (1988). *The Power of Myth.* New York: Doubleday. Xvii, 217-230.

Fiore, C., Landsburg, A. (1979). *Death Encounters.* New York: Bantam. 171.

Flynn, C. (1982). Meanings and implications of NDE Transformations: Some preliminary Findings and implications. Anabiosid. 2, (1), 4-7.

Flynn, C. (1986). *After the Beyond.* New Jersey: Prentice Hall.

Frankel, V.E. (1965). *Man's Search for Meaning.* New York: Washington Square Press. xii.

Geraci, J.K. (1990). Near-Death Survivors and How Their Loss of Fear of Death Relates to Wellness. Unpublished manuscript, Central Connecticut State University.

Greyson, B. (1981). Near Death Experiences and Attempted Suicides, Suicide and Life-Threatening Behavior. 11, (1), 10-16.

Greyson, B. (1983). The Near-Death Experiences and Personal Values.

Journal of Psychiatry. 140, (5),619.

Gross, P.R., Levitt, N., Lewis, M.W. (1996). The Flight from Science and Reason.

New York: New York Academy of Sciences. 494-498, 563-569.

Levine, S. (1997). *A year to Live.* New York: Bell Tower.

Reinhold, M. (1949). *Classics Greek and Roman.* New York: Barron's Educational Series.

Ring, K. (1984). *Heading Toward Omega.*

Ross, E.K. (1969). *On Death and Dying.* New York: Macmillan. 15.

Spradley, J.P. (1979). *The Ethnographic Interview.* New York: Holt Rhinehart and Winston.

Taylor, D. (1981). Profile of an Experiencer. Vital Signs. 1-6.

Whitton, J.L., Fisher, J. (1986). *Life Between Life.* New York, Warner Books.

Young, A.M. (1984). Are the Foundations of Science Adequate? ReVISION. 7, (1), 5-15.

About the Author

~

Dr. Geraci is a former decorated police officer, educator and adjunct professor of psychology and death and dying. He holds a master's degree in psychology from Central Connecticut State University, Certificate of Advanced Graduate Study from the University of Hartford, and a Ph.D. in Educational Studies from the University of Connecticut.

He had his near-death experience in 1977. It wasn't until years later that he shared it with family and friends. As time went on, he shared it publicly through the media and lectures. Now, 44 years later, he has chosen to reflect on his experience and its effect on his life. He is retired and enjoys spending time in nature and with his children, grandchildren and great grandchildren.

www.ingramcontent.com/pod-product-compliance
Lightning Source LLC
LaVergne TN
LVHW090116080426
835507LV00040B/911